CONSTRUCTION LAW

IN A NUTSHELL®

by

DONALD E. CAMPBELL
Associate Professor of Law
Mississippi College School of Law

WEST
ACADEMIC
PUBLISHING

© 2015 LEG, Inc. d/b/a West Academic

   444 Cedar Street, Suite 700
   St. Paul, MN 55101
   1-877-888-1330

West, West Academic Publishing, and West Academic are trademarks of West Publishing Corporation, used under license.

Printed in the United States of America

ISBN: 978-1-62810-107-2

PREFACE

Construction law has been around since a caveman put one rock on top of another for shelter and the structure collapsed maiming a neighbor. Then, the dispute was surely resolved in favor of the stronger of the two combatants (under the venerable legal doctrine of "might makes right"). However, despite these ancient origins, and its development into a unique and respected area of the law today, law schools have been late to consider construction law on its own terms. Ironically, this is not true for other professional schools—such as architecture and construction management—which have made construction law a core part of the curriculum. This is all changing, however, and this book is a testament to that change.

The goal of this book is to provide the reader a foundational understanding of the players and legal disputes that can arise in a construction project. Of course the more complex the project the more complex the problems, but even in the simplest construction or renovation disputes arise, and the parties need to know their legal rights and obligations. This book is an overview of those rights and obligations.

This book takes each of the primary participants in a construction project and examines the legal doctrines applicable to that participant. The players analyzed are the owner, contractor, design professional, subcontractor, and surety. In addition to these chapters there are also chapters discussing common contractual provisions, defective construction, the economic loss rule, and damages. This structure is intentional and hopefully provides a way to organize a syllabus or course of study that is not only chronological but also intuitive.

This book has been a labor of love. I enjoy reading, writing, and teaching about construction law. However, there is no such thing as a perfect manuscript or approach, and I certainly do not claim perfection here. Decisions had to be made about what to put in and what to leave out (it is a nutshell after all) and where to put concepts that could cross-cut chapters. I encourage the reader to provide feedback and comments that will serve to improve future editions of the book.

In closing, I would like to provide a thank-you to several folks. First to my research assistants that helped me gather cases and materials as I wrote, and particular Mr. Russell Dumas who provided the final push needed to get the book finalized. I would also like to thank two folks with West Academic— Ms. Elaine Thompson who first planted the seed for this project and Mac Soto who gently but firmly pushed me toward completion of the book for their guidance. A continuing thanks to the administration at MC Law, particularly Dean Scott and Dean Emeritus Rosenblatt, who are a constant source of support and encouragement. Finally, but certainly not least, I thank those who have taken my construction law class. Without them, this book would not exist.

DONALD E. CAMPBELL

May 1, 2015

OUTLINE

TABLE OF CASES

References are to Pages

CONSTRUCTION LAW

LAW

IN A NUTSHELL®

CHAPTER 1

INTRODUCTION TO CONSTRUCTION LAW

A. SOURCES OF CONSTRUCTION LAW

Construction law implicates several sources of law. While the rights and obligations of those involved in a construction project are primarily governed by the terms of their contracts, it would be incorrect to think of construction law merely as advanced contracts. As one court noted, construction disputes "are a separate breed of animal."[1] In fact, even in the realm of contracts, there are a number of doctrines and provisions unique to the construction industry. In addition to contracts, statutes and municipal codes, tort law, and constitutional law all contribute to an understanding of the area. With this many rules and regulations implicating even the simplest construction project, it is not surprising that a number of states have certifications available for lawyers who specialize in construction law.

Statutes and municipal ordinances place numerous obligations and restrictions on parties to a construction contract. It is impossible to give a comprehensive list, but to give a sense of their importance, consider federal and state environmental statutes, bidding, and workplace safety laws; state licensing laws, lien right laws,

---

[1]   Paul Hardeman, Inc. v. Arkansas Power & Light Co., 380 F.Supp. 298, 317 (E.D. Ark. 1974).

and laws of limitation/repose; and local zoning ordinances and building codes. Jurisdiction-specific variations add to the complexity.

Tort law also impacts the construction process. Negligent misrepresentation—an allegation that material information was not provided or was incorrect—is a common claim. Suits for defective construction and personal injury as a result of worksite conditions also arise. In addition, claims of professional malpractice are asserted against architects or engineers for inadequate plans or designs. Often, construction contracts attempt to address potential tort liability through clauses that allocate or limit risk, but there are situations where those provisions prove inadequate or unenforceable. For claimants, the economic loss rule—a rule designed to maintain the divide between contract and tort remedies—may also bar an otherwise valid claim.

Finally, construction law implicates state and federal constitutional law. These claims are likely to revolve around due process rights—particularly with regard to issues of payment. For example, Mississippi had a statute which gave subcontractors the right to provide notice to an owner that the subcontractor has not been paid by the contractor and imposed a lien on the funds in the owner's hands (called a Stop Notice Statute), which the Fifth Circuit Court of Appeals held violated the Fifth Amendment of the United States Constitution. The court held the statute deprived the contractor of property without sufficient procedural safeguards (*i.e.* lack of a judicial hearing prior to a taking of the funds).[2]

B. ROLE AND IMPORTANCE OF STANDARDIZED INDUSTRY CONTRACT FORMS (AIA, AGC, EJCDC)

Contractual relationships are the foundation of a construction project. There is likely no other endeavor where so many contracts are both separate and interrelated at the same time. To understand what this means, consider a simple hypothetical. Owner wishes to construct a building, so she contracts with an architect to prepare plans and specifications. After the design is complete, Owner contracts with a general contractor to build the structure consistent with the architect's design. The general contractor then contracts with subcontractors to perform the work.

This simple construction project includes three separate and distinct contractual relationships. The owner does not have a relationship with the subcontractor who is doing the work on site. The subcontractor does not have a relationship with the owner who is the party that ultimately must be pleased with the completed project. The general contractor does not have a contract with the designer whose plans and specifications the contractor is seeking to implement.

---

[2]   Noatex Corp. v. King Const. of Houston, LLC, 732 F.3d 479 (5th Cir. 2013).

It should be easy to see how these intimately-related but separate contractual relationships can result in conflict and dispute. Owner is interested in making sure that the subcontractor performs pursuant to the building design even though they lack a contractual relationship. To do this, Owner needs to ensure that contractual obligations between subcontractor and contractor are consistent with contractor's obligations to the Owner. To deal with the overlapping nature of the relationships and to reduce the number of disputes that arise, parties often utilize one of a handful of standardized contracts drafted by industry groups. These forms contain standard terms and conditions that can be modified to address unique aspects of a particular project. The contracts are intended both to provide consistency across the various relationships and to address common issues that arise in the course of a project. Not only do these form contracts provide an opportunity to save time and money, but they also provide those executing the project the comfort of knowing what to expect because they have likely operated under the same terms in prior projects.

Three groups have proposed the most popular model agreements—the American Institute of Architects (AIA), the Associated General Contractors (AGC), and the Engineers Joint Contract Documents Committee (EJCDC). While each of these sets of documents purports to strive for a fair application of rights and obligations among the parties to a project, it is important to remember that the contracts are drafted by industry groups with a constituency motivated to protect their interests as much as possible in the terms of the agreements.

The AIA documents, which are revised approximately every 10 years (with the last revision in 2007), historically have been the most popular set of documents and will be the exemplar analyzed in this book. However, there are a liberal sprinkling of citations to other standardized documents as well. The reasons the AIA documents continue to be the most popular include their longevity and familiarity as well as the fact that one of the first contracts entered into on a project is with the design professional—commonly an architect—who is likely to propose the AIA documents to the owner. Structurally, the standardized contracts are divided into different series or categories of documents based on the parties involved and the type of delivery system or payment method involved. For example, with the AIA documents, the Owner-Contractor contracts are designated as "A-Series"; the "B-Series" documents are those between the owner and the architect; and the "C-Series" agreements are those between an architect and other design professionals (such as engineers). The "G-Series" provides a set of form documents that are contemplated under the other Series to carry out the project, such as change orders and applications for payment.

In addition to their longevity and familiarity, form contracts possess certain other advantages that make them popular. First, notwithstanding the fact that self-interested groups draft them, they are largely thought to be fair (after all, contracts with highly skewed or preferential terms would begin to find a smaller and smaller following). Second, the parties are familiar with the general terms of these contracts and can focus negotiation on project-specific concerns or specific problematic terms within the contracts. Third, they possess an element of consistency integrating the contracts between other parties. Finally, the form contracts contain many terms that could easily be overlooked by parties drafting a contract from scratch.

While these advantages make the standard from contracts attractive options, there are a few downsides worth noting. The contracts are "standard" which means the terms will not have taken into account the laws from any particular jurisdiction, and any peculiarities of that jurisdiction will need to be addressed separately. Also, as noted, self-interested groups draft the forms, so some of the provisions may evince a bias toward that group or may omit terms preferred by the other party. There also may be specific needs in a project not addressed by any of the standard forms. Finally, there is a risk that the forms may lull an attorney into accepting terms that are not beneficial to the client.

C. GENERAL RULES OF CONTRACT FORMATION AND INTERPRETATION

The general rules of contract formation and interpretation apply to construction contracts. These rules are not unique to the construction process but are important to understand when interpreting a particular contractual provision.

Parties to a construction contract may wish to commence work on the project prior to the finalization of a contract. An owner might be particularly anxious to begin construction for personal or financial reasons. Similarly, a design professional, contractor, or subcontractor might be inclined to begin early to demonstrate expertise and ability or to create pressure on the owner to finalize the whole contract. Taking action prior to having agreement on all terms can compromise not only the working relationship between the parties but also result in performance of work with no right to payment or at most a *quantum meruit* recovery. Another potential risk of beginning work without a contract in place is that either party can stop the work at any time without notice.

When the owner or contractor start construction on a project prior to entering into a fully integrated and complete contract, they may enter into a **letter of intent (LOI)**. This is an agreement between the parties to continue negotiations on the primary contract but allow work to commence. At its core, a LOI should be an authorization to perform work and in the event a complete contract cannot be reached, provisions for that the party performing the work to be paid for the work performed. The benefit of an LOI is that it provides for an earlier start to the project than might otherwise be possible. The risk, however, is that the letter can lead to costly and time-consuming disputes. The LOI that includes a clause explicitly contemplating a more formal agreement in the future may create ambiguity as to exactly what the parties intended—was the purpose of the letter to bind the parties to the terms of the LOI or merely an indication of on-going negotiations? To give an example, consider *Quake Const. v. American Airlines.*[3] In that case, the general contractor in an airport project sent an LOI to a subcontractor to authorize commencement of some work. The LOI stated that the overall contract would be available "shortly" and that the LOI could be cancelled if no agreement was reached. The contractor subsequently terminated the subcontractor before any work began, and the subcontractor sued arguing that the letter of intent was sufficiently specific to create an enforceable contract. The trial court dismissed the suit holding that the parties agreed not to be bound until the final agreement was reached. The intermediate appellate court and the Illinois Supreme Court found that there was ambiguity in the letter because the terms indicated both that the parties did not intend to be bound (the provision that the contractor could terminate at any time) and an intent to be bound (stating that the subcontract would be available "shortly" and allowing for cancellation), and remanded the case for trial. Regardless of the outcome, the costs of an early start may outweigh its benefits.

---

[3]   565 N.E. 2d 990 (Ill. 1990).

1. CONTRACT FORMATION: OFFER, ACCEPTANCE, AND CONSIDERATION

To have a valid and enforceable contract, there must be an offer, acceptance and consideration. An **offer** is an expression of a willingness to enter into a contract that is sufficiently definite in the essential terms of the deal that if accepted, is enforceable.[4] **Acceptance** is a manifestation of assent to being bound to the terms as set out in the offer.[5] In the construction industry, a contractor's bid or estimate is considered an offer. For example, Contractor provides Owner a bid to build Owner's house (an offer). Owner might accept the offer as proposed by Contractor. Upon acceptance, there would be a contract formed. Owner, however, might also change some of the terms of the offer and send it back to Contractor. In that situation the bid with the changed terms would be considered a **counter-offer**, and would not bind either Owner or Contractor.[6] The acceptance must be on the same terms that were offered. Only when the parties come to a **"meeting of the mind"** with regard to the same terms is an enforceable contract formed— therefore, counter-offers and **preliminary negotiations** do not establish a contract.

The general rule with regard to offers is that they can be withdrawn any time prior to acceptance.[7] This general rule, however, finds an exception in the

---

[4]   Restatement (Second) of Contracts § 24.

[5]   Restatement (Second) of Contracts § 50.

[6]   Restatement (Second) of Contracts § 50.

[7]   Restatement (Second) of Contracts § 42.

construction context. Consider a situation where a contractor bids on a project—with the amount of the bid based on quotes from a subcontractor. Under the general rule, the subcontractor could withdraw the quote provided to (and relied upon by the) contractor any time prior to the contractor being awarded the project and accepting the subcontractor's bid. Courts, recognizing the inequity that would result to the contractor if the subcontractor was able to withdraw the bid, developed a doctrine known as the **"firm bid"** rule. Under this doctrine, the subcontractor is bound—as a matter of equity (fairness)—to honor a quote that a contractor relies on in submitting a bid.[8]

In addition to an offer and acceptance, a valid, enforceable contract requires **consideration**. Consideration is the receipt of value or the giving up of something of value for a contract. Traditionally the consideration in a construction contract is the exchange of money for the construction of a project. Courts are hesitant to second-guess consideration and will often find value in a party either taking action or refraining from taking action.

2. ORAL CONTRACTS AND THE STATUTE OF FRAUDS

Generally, construction contracts do not have to be in writing to be valid. However, if a contract falls within the **Statute of Frauds** it must be in writing, contain the essential elements of the agreement,

---

[8]   Restatement (Second) of Contracts § 90. This concept is discussed in more detail in the Subcontractor Chapter.

and be signed by the party the contract is being enforced against. The statute of frauds—originally based on a statute passed by the English Parliament—is now either a statutory or common law doctrine in all jurisdictions of the United States. While states vary as to the precise types of contracts that are subject to the statute, two categories commonly included are relevant in the construction context. Contracts for the transfer of an interest in real property—including contracts for the sale of land and grant of an easement are subject to the statute. In addition, contracts that cannot be performed within one year must be in writing. For a contract to fall into this category there must be no possibility that the contract could be performed within a year. Therefore, where the contract is to build a house with no deadline for completion, the contract is not within the statute because it would be possible (even if not likely) to complete construction within a year.

3. INTERPRETING THE CONSTRUCTION CONTRACT

Industry groups drafted standardized contracts in an attempt to limit interpretation disputes by having uniform terms that apply across the various contracts in the construction process. Often, however, these forms may not be used, or may be used with individualized additions or modifications without considering the impact of the change on the rest of the contract, or the non-standardized provisions (such as the scope of work on a particular project) may contain ambiguities that require courts to interpret the language used.

These interpretation disputes presume a valid and enforceable contract. Contractual provisions range from extremely clear and beyond dispute to ambiguous and uncertain. If the terms are clear and unambiguous, courts will hold the parties to their bargain—even if it ultimately turns out that one party made a bad business decision in agreeing to the terms. And parties are prohibited from attempting to make a clear term ambiguous or modifying the contract with evidence outside the contract when the contract is fully integrated—that is, is the complete and final agreement. Often construction contracts will contain an **Integration Clause** that states that the contract is the full and complete agreement between the parties. The prohibition on using outside evidence to modify an integrated contract that is plain on its face is known as the **Parol Evidence Rule**.

All too often, however, contract language is not clear. Perhaps the contract was poorly drafted, unanticipated events call the meaning of a provision into question, or contractual provisions conflict. When these conflicts or ambiguities arise, courts are faced with having to interpret the terms. A court's ultimate goal is to identify the intent of the parties and to respect that intent. To aid in this task, courts have developed several doctrines of contract interpretation. The most important of these in the construction context are discussed below.

a. Interpretation Against Drafter (*contra proferentem*)

In determining how to interpret an ambiguous term, courts will interpret it against the drafter of the contract. The justification for this rule is that the drafter had the power to protect itself by clear drafting. For example, where a contractor drafted a subcontract, and the payment term was ambiguous as to whether the subcontractor was entitled to payment only after the contractor received payment from the owner or whether the subcontractor was entitled to payment regardless of whether the owner paid the contractor, the court adopted the interpretation that favored the non-drafting subcontractor.[9]

b. Favor Interpretation That Gives Meaning to Entire Agreement

When faced with two competing interpretations of a provision—one which renders other provisions of a contract inoperative and another which allows all terms to retain meaning—courts will favor the latter interpretation. Because construction contracts often include numerous separate documents and contracts incorporate by reference agreements of other parties, this doctrine has particular relevance.

---

[9]   *Mrozik Construction, Inc. v. Lovering Associates, Inc.*, 461 N.W.2d 49 (Minn. App. Ct. 1990).

c. Specific Prevails over General Terms and Written Prevails over Printed Terms

In attempting to identify the intent of the parties, specific contractual terms are considered to be more reliable evidence of intent than general terms. Similarly, written terms are considered better evidence of the parties' intent than printed provisions. These doctrines are important in the construction context where parties may enter into form contracts—without really knowing or understanding what the forms contain—and then negotiate new terms that conflict with the provisions of the form contract. For example, where a residential construction contract contained a handwritten warranty term on the front and a less generous warranty provision in the boilerplate typed provisions on the back of the contract, the court held the longer handwritten warranty applied.[10]

d. Course of Performance and Prior Dealings

Because the ultimate goal of a court in interpreting an ambiguous contract is to determine the intent of the contracting parties, if the parties have had prior dealings, courts will consider evidence of those prior dealings in determining intent. This includes both prior dealings in separate contracts as well as prior dealings over the course of performance on a single project.

---

[10]   *Montgomery Ward & Co. v. Dalton*, 665 S.W.2d 507 (Tex. App. El Paso 1983).

e. Custom and Usage in Trade

Reliance on custom and usage within the relevant industry is also used to interpret an ambiguous term or to serve as a gap-filler when a contract is silent as to an obligation. This approach is considered less reliable than course of performance/prior dealings (which provides evidence of the intent of these particular parties). However, where a custom or usage is established and of general knowledge within a particular field, courts may consider it. For example, where a contract required a contractor to paint "all previously painted or varnished surfaces", and the owner asserted this required the contractor to paint enameled surfaces, the court looked to the meaning of the phrase "enameled surfaces" within the painting industry. The court ultimately determined that in industry usage the phase did not contemplate the painting of enameled surfaces, adopting the contractor's interpretation.[11]

D.   THIRD-PARTY BENEFICIARIES

Individuals are generally only liable to those with whom they have a contractual relationship. Therefore, typically an owner is not contractually responsible to a subcontractor and a design professional is not contractually obligated to a contractor. This could create problems when, for example, the subcontractor has not been paid by the

---

[11]   *Gholson, Byars & Holmes Const. Co. v. U.S.*, 351 F.2d 987 (Ct. Cl. 1965).

contractor while the owner receives the benefit of the subcontractor's work.

In these situations, a party may claim they have a right to recover against someone they do not have a contractual relationship with as a **third-party beneficiary**. Thus, in the example above, the subcontractor may attempt to claim that he is a third-party beneficiary of the contract between the owner and contractor in order to assert payment rights against the owner.

In most jurisdictions it is very difficult for a non-party to a contract to succeed on a third-party beneficiary claim. The third-party beneficiary doctrine is intended to allow those who were the object of the underlying contract to assert rights under the contract. This can be shown by evidence that the contracting parties intended to benefit the third-party in their contract or that the third-party was intended to be the beneficiary of the contract between the parties. It is not enough that the third-party be an incidental beneficiary to the contract. The contract between the owner and the contractor is to complete the project and not to benefit the subcontractor (and the contract between the owner and the architect is to prepare designs and not to benefit the contractor); and therefore courts generally hold that non-contracting parties are not third-party beneficiaries in the construction context.

E.   CONCLUSION

The remainder of this book will discuss the major players in a construction project and the legal issues that can arise with each. This will include the owner, design professional, contractor, and subcontractor, and surety. These of course are not all of those that influence a construction project. Other players include lenders, insurance companies, and governments at all levels. These players are discussed as they impact the major participants in the project. It should also be noted that these are "minor" players only in how the discussion is organized. An owner that is dependent on financing from a lender to begin construction certainly does not consider the lender a minor participant.

CHAPTER 2

THE ROLE OF THE OWNER

The owner in a construction project is the individual or entity for whom the construction is performed. The owner may be a private or public entity. While all owners ultimately desire a completed project, their motivation and expectations for the project can have a significant impact on the nature of the relationships between the parties to the project. An owner could be motivated primarily by cost, functionality, aesthetics, or quality. Public projects also implicate issues of protection of the public treasury and prevention of corruption. The owner has a number of responsibilities both before and during the construction process. This chapter addresses those obligations.

A. PRE-CONSTRUCTION OBLIGATIONS

1. SELECTION OF SITE

The owner must select the site where construction will occur, ensure legal authority to build on the location, and ensure that the project is feasible in the location. Throughout this book, the word "owner" is used to mean the person/entity who desires to have something built. It does not necessarily entail the fee simple owner of the property. A tenant, whose lease with the landlord provides the legal right to construct a building, is the owner even though the tenant is not the record owner of the property. The owner has an obligation to ensure that she has the legal right to build on the location. In addition, the owner has an obligation to obtain the initial permits and approvals necessary for construction to commence.

Even if the owner has the legal right to build, there could be other restrictions that limit what can be built in a location. Federal, state and municipal zoning, land use, and environmental laws may limit the types of structures constructed in an area (or whether construction can be commenced at all). In addition to these regulatory restrictions, the property may also be burdened by private restrictions—such as easements or restrictive covenants. Easements on the property may limit where or how a structure is built. Restrictive covenants may limit several aspects of construction. For example, residential subdivision covenants may contain restrictions on where construction vehicles can travel during construction, setback or minimum square footage requirements, restrictions on the type of construction materials or design features that can be built on the property.

The physical condition of the site may also limit construction. The owner must ensure that the site itself is suitable for construction of the building the owner wants. To do this, the owner may retain a geotechnical engineer to evaluate subsurface conditions and/or an environmental consultant to evaluate whether there are any environmental hazards on the site.

2.   SELECTING THE DESIGN PROFESSIONAL

Owners have a vision for a structure but rarely have the expertise to prepare the construction documents that lead to a completed project, and so they retain a design professional to assist in preparing the plans and specifications. The two primary types of design professionals are architects and engineers. Whether the owner retains an architect or engineer depends on the type of structure. Architects traditionally prepare designs for structures used or occupied by people. For public works projects such as water treatment plants or bridges, an engineer may be the lead design professional.

Whether a project is public or private has significant implications on how the design professional is selected. An owner on a private project is free to negotiate with the design professional of its choosing—based on whatever criteria the owner considers the most important. On the other hand, public owners must always be conscious of statutory procurement requirements and limitations.

Public procurement statutes recognize that design professional selection implicates different concerns than contractor selection. While the public's interest in contractor selection is primarily to obtain the lowest cost to the taxpayers, the same may not be true for design professionals. With regard to the design, the primary goal may be to find a professional with a certain amount of experience or a particular reputation or design style. A selection approach based on the lowest bid would often undermine these goals. Public procurement statutes attempt both to overcome this problem while at the same time attempting to lessen the opportunity for corruption in the selection process.

In the federal system, the standard for selecting the design professional is set out in a statute known as the **Brooks Act**. 40 U.S.C. §§ 1101–1104. State statutes that follow the federal practice (although often modified in some aspects) are commonly known as **Little Brooks Acts**. The Brooks Act requires federal agencies to publicly announce the requirements for architectural or engineering services, and encourage firms to submit statements of qualifications and performance. The agency must consult with discuss design options with at least three firms, and must order the three in order of "most highly qualified." Using this listing, the agency begins negotiations with the highest ranked firm to obtain a "fair and reasonable" price which is determined by the nature of the project. If the agency is unable to finalize a contract with the first firm on its list, it moves to the next firm and continues in this manner until an agreement is reached.

3.   SELECTING THE CONTRACTOR

The owner will also select the contractor to perform the work. How the contractor is selected will depend on the type of project involved—whether private or public. While the discussion below focuses on the distinction between public and private contracting, it should be noted that there has been a proliferation of projects in which the private sector and public sector partner. The nature of these relationships are numerous. Generally, whether the project is identified as public or private depends on how the project is funded (the more public funds the more likely it will be considered public) and ultimate control of the project (the more public control the more likely it is that the project will be considered public).

a. Public Bidding Selection Process

Selection of a contractor on public projects is regulated by state and federal procurement laws. Most often, public bodies are required by law to utilize a design-bid-build project delivery system. This means that the owner must first develop the design and specifications for the project, then accept bids from contractors to build the project. The goal of this selection approach is three-fold. First, to ensure that the public is getting the best deal for its money. To this end, public statutes prefer selection of the lowest bid submitted. Second, to protect against owners relying on improper factors to select a contractor (*e.g.* favoritism). This is accomplished through the use of a sealed bidding process. The third goal is to ensure that the contractor selected has the capacity to perform the contract. This is accomplished by allowing public bodies to consider the responsibility of a contractor in addition to the amount of the bid.

The initial action by the public entity is to issue an **invitation for bids** or **request for proposals**. The invitation provides instructions and guidance for contractors who desire to bid on the project. To this end, the invitation will discuss the project, any special instructions (such as the requirement for bid security), and information about when and when and where bids are to be submitted and when they will be opened.

If, after reading an invitation for bids, a contractor wishes to bid on a project, he/she will obtain a copy of the documents needed to prepare a bid. The invitation for bids will contain information on where the contractor can obtain the **bid package** for the project. The bid package contains a copy of the plans and specifications and the contract for the project as well as any relevant instructions for preparing the bid. It may also contain any reports or analysis that the owner had prepared prior to seeking bids.

i. Sealed Bidding Process and the Responsive Bids

Public projects utilize a sealed bidding process. As part of the process, the invitation for bids contains a precise time that bids must be received and a time that they will be opened. Bids not submitted by the deadline are considered non-responsive and will be rejected (or subject to a bid protest if accepted). States may have special requirements that, if not met, will require rejection of a bid before it is opened. For example, in Mississippi, a contractor must include a valid license number placed on the outside of their bid, and if it is not present the bid may not be opened or considered.[1] A contractor must be diligent to follow the specific requirements of the relevant procurement statute as well as the invitation to bid.

A bid that is not strictly in compliance with the instructions for completing and submitting a bid is considered non-responsive. A public body may only award a project to a **responsive** bidder. A non-responsive bid contains an error or omission that is significant enough to give the bidder an unfair advantage in the bidding process. Whether a bid is responsive occurs along a continuum. On one end of the spectrum is a bid that conforms precisely to the bid instructions. On the other end of the spectrum are those errors or omissions that clearly give the bidder an unfair advantage or that require rejection of the bid as a matter of statute. For example, a bid that fails to include in the bid the cost of a portion of the project would render a bid non-responsive.

In the middle of the continuum are bid irregularities that do not trigger the same concerns about unfairness but contain discrepancies, errors or omissions with what was required by the bid package. These irregularities do not impact the substance of the contract (i.e. they do not significantly impact the price, quantity, quality or delivery of the project), but are a failure to follow a formality of the bid documents. The question is

---

[1]   Miss. Code Ann. § 31–3–21(1).

whether these type of errors and omissions are a **material deviation** that cannot be waived or are a non-material deviation which will not prevent the owner from awarding the project to the bidder. This raises the question of what precisely is a "material" versus "non-material" (insignificant) omission. While certain irregularities may be designated as material by the bid package, statute, or court decisions, when the omission does not fall within one of these categories, the decision of whether to accept or reject the bid is left largely to the discretion of the public owner. Reviewing courts will not overturn the decision to award the contract based on a non-material deviation unless the decision is arbitrary or capricious.

ii. Lowest Responsible Bid

A fundamental aspect of the public bidding process is that the owner must award the project to the lowest responsive and responsible bidder. The "lowest" part of the equation is straight forward. The lowest bid is the one that is the least dollar amount when the bids are opened. If, after opening all bids, there are none within the proscribed budget, the public owner may elect to reject all bids and choose whether to re-issue an invitation for bids. The responsive element is discussed above— and requires the bidder to materially comply with the bid requirements. The third requirement is that the bidder be "responsible." Public funds are not protected if a contractor is awarded a contract because they had the lowest bid, but is thereafter unable or unwilling to complete the project—

causing taxpayers to incur the cost in time and money of having the project completed by another contractor. Procurement laws give public bodies discretion to consider not only the amount of the bid but also the quality of the contractor submitting the bid. This is often termed identifying the lowest **responsible bidder**.

Owners evaluate the responsibility of a contractor by considering several factors that indicate that the contractor can be relied upon to complete the project. These factors include, but are not limited to: financial stability, past performance on similar projects, and reputation. Consideration of responsibility may require independent investigation by the public owner and is completed prior to awarding the contract.

iii. Bid Protests

Bidders not awarded a project have the right to file a **bid protest**. The protester may believe that the winning bid was unresponsive or that the winning bidder was not responsible. As a matter of procedure, the protest must be filed within the proscribed time frame and with the appropriate body or the protester risks losing the right to challenge the award. Statutes or regulations often establish a very short time frame for bringing a challenge. The protester must also file the protest in the proper location. By statute or regulation, the appropriate venue may be either with an agency or directly to a court for review.

Pursuing a bid protest may not be worth the time and money for two primary reasons. First, courts give agencies great deference in evaluating a bidder's responsiveness and responsibility. Second, even if the protest is successful, it is rare that a reviewing body will award the protester more than bid preparation costs if the contract has already been executed. A protester may seek to enjoin construction of the project, but may have a difficult time establishing the elements necessary to obtain an injunction. Very few jurisdictions will award the protester lost profits from the project even if it is determined that the agency inappropriately awarded the contract.

b. Private Selection Process

A private owner has much more flexibility in selecting a contractor than a public owner. The owner may individually negotiate with a preferred contractor, without any bidding. The owner may also solicit bids. However, unlike in the public realm, a private owner is not obligated to accept the lowest bidder and may negotiate with the bidder of the owner's choice. Because a private owner is not limited to a bidding process, the owner can take advantage of approaches to selecting contractors other than the design-bid-build approach which is required by statute in the public realm.

4. SELECTING THE PROJECT DELIVERY SYSTEM

The **Project Delivery System** is the name given to the collective mechanism for designing, bidding, building, and paying for a project. On private projects, the owner decides the best delivery system to use. On public projects, the owner is limited in the delivery system options available by public bidding laws—typically to the traditional design-bid-build model.

Project delivery mechanisms (at least on private projects) are limited only by the imagination of the parties. However, over time, particular systems have become common and accepted approaches. Each of these primary approaches has unique benefits and drawbacks that the owner should consider.

a. Traditional Model (Design-Bid-Build)

The **Traditional Model**, also known as **Design-Bid-Build**, is the most common project delivery method. The owner contracts with a design professional to develop the design and specifications for a project. Once the design is complete, the owner selects a general contractor to construct the project (on public projects selecting the lowest responsive and responsible bidder). Often the design professional will assist in bid administration. After the contract is awarded, work commences, with the contractor either performing the work or retaining subcontractors to perform the work on the project. Under the standardized contract documents, the architect acts as the owner's agent on the job site, observing the progress of construction, responding to requests for design document clarification from the contractor, and certifying that the work is complete for payment.

There are a number of advantages to the traditional approach. There is a logic to the process by providing the owner with a complete design and the price of construction when construction commences. It also provides the owner with a great deal of control over the design team and the construction team—both of which have contractual obligations to the owner. In addition, this method also has the advantage of providing a sense of familiarity to the parties.

There are disadvantages to the traditional model, however. The order of the process is rigid, with construction coming only after the design is complete. This has downsides for the owner. First, the owner loses the opportunity to have someone familiar with the construction process involved at the design phase. Such involvement could assist the owner by providing design changes to save the owner money or identify potential design problems prior to commencement of construction. Second, construction is delayed until the design is complete. This may cause the owner to lose money either because of inflation (which could impact labor or material costs or interest rates) or because she has to forego the income from the project for a longer period of time than she would if design and construction could be going on simultaneously.

Finally, contractors have an incentive to cut costs and perhaps quality in order to submit the lowest bid to win the job. Similarly, contractors have an incentive to read the project specifications narrowly to reduce their bid and win the project, resulting in disputes after construction begins about what is within the scope of work under the contract and what is extra work that would entitle the contractor to additional compensation.

b. Design-Build

Design-build is a design delivery system in which both the design and construction is completed by one entity. A primary advantage of a design-build approach for an owner is consolidation of the responsibility for design and construction. This overcomes two primary drawbacks of the traditional approach. First, if the owner wishes, the construction phase can begin before the design is complete. Second, it provides an opportunity for the owner to avoid contractor claims based on defective or inadequate design documents. Under the traditional model, because the design documents are prepared by the design professional on behalf of the owner, the owner remains liable for inadequacies in the design documents. This is not true with design-build, where the designer and contractor are one and the same. In addition, the inclusion of construction expertise at the design phase can result in a savings to the owner through **value engineering**—incorporating lower cost approaches into the plans and specifications without compromising the functionality or quality of the project. The contractor (who actually performs the work) may be more familiar with these value engineering options than the design professional.

The design build approach has its drawbacks for the owner however. Because the nature of the relationship between the owner and the design-build team is not an agency relationship, an owner must have enough sophistication to provide sufficient detail to the team to ensure that the project is designed and built within budget and consistent with the owner's aesthetic goals. An owner that cannot provide this information up front may have to incur the additional cost of retaining consultants independent of the design build team to assist with development of the initial concept.

c. Construction Management

A construction management delivery system is an umbrella term for a variety of design delivery systems. While the term construction manager does not have a set meaning, generally construction management delivery systems can be divided into two distinct categories based on the responsibilities assumed by the construction manager. The first is the **agency construction manager** and the second is the **construction manager at-risk.** Consistent with both types of construction management structures is the involvement of individuals familiar with construction early in the process. The early involvement allows an owner to rely on the construction manager's expertise in developing the design, and to ensure, with an eye toward construction, that the design documents are consistent to eliminate discrepancies and that the project is constructible within budget and on time. A construction manager's involvement also provides **value engineering** input. The construction manager's presence may also allow initial phases of construction to begin prior to finalization of the design. The primary distinctions between the two types of construction management delivery systems are where risk for project design and construction rests. Unlike the design-bid-build delivery system, contract management firms are traditionally not selected based on a low bid, but are instead selected based on reputation or experience.

i. Agency Construction Manager

As first conceptualized, the construction management approach contemplated that an owner would retain a construction manager for a fixed amount to serve as the owner's agent from the design stage through the end of construction. This is known as **agency construction manager.** This approach provides the advantage of having a construction specialist involved early in the project. The construction manager serves as the owner's eyes and ears—its agent—both during design and construction.

During the preconstruction stage, the agency construction manager provides the owner with advice on designing with an eye toward construction. This may mean catching discrepancies in the plans or specifications that could arise in the construction process (and lead to disputes or change orders) and providing value engineering. During the construction phase, the construction manager assists the owner with selection of subcontractors and coordinates the trades.

As the agency construction manager approach matured, owners began to realize that the delivery system failed to do an adequate job of eliminating an owner's primary concern—increased costs on a project. While the agency relationship provided advice that the owner sought, the relationship did nothing to shift liability away from the owner when the project faced budget-busting cost overages or delays. The structure of the relationship means that the owner maintains responsibilities that would generally fall to a general contractor—such as direct contractual relationships with subcontractors and responsibility for a project's late completion. This led owners to look for a delivery mechanism that not only made design and construction components more efficient, but also shifted as much risk as possible away from the owner.

ii. Construction Manager At-Risk (CMAR)

Owners, concerned about the risk of liability with Agency Construction Managers, began to consider an alternative delivery system: **Construction Manager At-Risk**. The construction manager at-risk becomes involved early in the project and assists the owner with development of the design, just like an agency construction manager, and during this preconstruction phase the advantages of the construction manager are the same. Once the construction phase begins, however, the construction manager at-risk plays a role similar to that of a general contractor in a design-bid-build system. The construction manager at-risk provides the owner with a proposal or quote for a fixed amount to complete construction of the project and then enters into contracts with subcontractors. While this is similar to the design-bid-build approach, the fact that the construction manager has been involved in review of the design documents and has likely solicited subcontractor review regarding constructability of the design, means that subcontractors selected are more likely to be familiar with the project and less likely to dispute the design during construction. Another characteristic that makes this relationship unique is the fact that the construction manager (unlike the general contractor) may stand in a position of trust with the owner. For example, in the AIA contract, the relationship is described as one of "trust and confidence."[2]

The primary difference between the at-risk and agency construction manager is the shift in risk from the owner to the construction manager. The construction manager is responsible for unjustified delays and defective construction. The construction manager also assumes responsibility for claims from subcontractors—providing a layer of protection for the owner which is not present in an agency construction manager approach.

---

[2]   AIA A133–2009 § 1.2.

d. Multi-Prime Contracting

The owner may choose to serve as its own general contractor. This delivery system is known as **multi-prime contracting**. In this system the owner contracts and coordinates with different trades on a project. By eliminating the general contractor, the owner can avoid the profit increase that a general contractor would include with each trade's work. Unsurprisingly, a primary disadvantage is that it places an owner in a position in which it is responsible for the obligations and liability that a general contractor would ordinarily assume. Thus, the owner is responsible for coordination and site access for all trades and assumes responsibilities that would ordinarily fall upon the general contractor.

5.   SELECTING THE PRICING METHOD

In selecting the project delivery system, an owner must also take into account how the project will be paid for. There are four primary methods of pricing the contract. The type of pricing and payment structure may be determined by the type of project or may be driven by the amount of risk the owner or contractor is willing to assume. This section addresses selection of pricing mechanism for the project as a whole. Other sections address pricing and payment issues that arise during the course of the project.[3] It should also be noted that parties can utilize more than one type of pricing method on the

---

[3]   Cite to the chapter dealing with dispute resolution during the course of the project.

same project, and although the discussion below talks in terms of owner and contractor, contracts between contractors and subcontractors/suppliers also use these pricing arrangements.

a. Fixed-Price

A **fixed-price** contract is the most common pricing method, and is often preferred or required by statute in public construction contracts. In a fixed-price contract the owner provides detailed specifications and the contractor submits a fixed quote to perform the work.[4] Under this approach, the owner has certainty as to cost of the project and the contractor has certainty as to the scope of the work the contractor is obligated to perform. It should be apparent that this pricing mechanism places the risk largely on the contractor. While the contractor may be entitled to additional compensation for work added after the contract is signed, with regard to the scope of work set out in the contract, the contractor is agreeing to perform for the set amount even if the cost of labor or supplies increases over the course of the project. The flip is also true. If the contractor is able to work efficiently and save money on a project, the contractor receives the increased profit and not the owner.

This pricing method creates tension and the opportunity for disputes. The contractor has an incentive to do the work as quickly and cheaply as

---

[4]   A101–2007 4.3.

possible to realize a maximum amount of profit, and has an incentive to read any ambiguity in the contract documents as justifying a cheaper/quicker construction method. The owner, on the other hand, certain of the maximum payment for the scope of work, has an incentive to argue that the contract documents demand better materials or craftsmanship. The contractor also has an incentive to argue that certain work is outside the contractual scope of work to justify an increase in the contract amount, while the owner has the incentive to argue that it is within the scope of work to avoid additional costs.

b. Cost-Plus

A **cost-plus** payment method is defined by its name. The owner pays the contractor for the cost of construction (labor, materials, etc.), plus a set amount for overhead and profit, which is usually a percentage of the cost of the project.[5] This approach has an advantage over a fixed-price approach because construction can begin before the project design is completed.

Because the owner is responsible for the contractor's "costs," establishing clearly within the contract the definition of costs is critical. Consider the situation where the contractor hires a supervisor to stay on site to coordinate the work. Is the supervisor's salary a cost that the contractor can pass on to the owner, or is it an expense the

---

[5] AIA 103–2007 5.1.

contractor should have to absorb into the "plus" part of the fee? What about when the contractor uses her own forces to perform work instead of a subcontractor? What if the contractor receives a discount on purchase of items incorporated into the project (perhaps because he purchased in bulk), is the full price the "cost" to be passed on to the owner or the discounted amount? The more detailed the definition of costs, the fewer the disputes between the owner and contractor. Standardized contracts anticipate these disputes and address the most common issues that arise by setting out what is and is not considered reimbursable "costs".[6]

The cost-plus pricing method affords the owner the risks/benefits that the fixed price method provided the contractor. The owner runs the risk that the cost of the project will be beyond what the owner budgeted. However, the owner also receives the benefit if the costs of the project are less than anticipated. The contractor, on the other hand, has an incentive to push up the cost of the project thereby increasing the amount recovered by the contractor in the "plus" portion of the contract. So, for example, a contractor may have an incentive to retain a costly subcontractor. This means that the owner must assume the additional responsibility (and cost) of supervision to ensure the project is being completed in an efficient manner and that the contractor has adequately documented its costs. Standardize contracts seek to place on the contractor an obligation not to unnecessarily run up

---

[6]   AIA A103–2007.

costs by stating that the costs must be reasonable or necessary and that the contractor will perform the work in "an expeditious and economical manner consistent with the owner's interests."[7]

c. Cost-Plus with Guaranteed Maximum Price

A major drawback of the cost-plus pricing method from the owner's standpoint is that the owner is contractually obligated to pay the cost of the project, without certainty as to what that ultimate amount will be. To obtain the flexibility of the cost-plus contract and the pricing certainty of the fixed-price approach, an owner may opt for **cost-plus with guaranteed maximum price**.[8] The definition of this pricing structure is in the name. The owner agrees to pay cost-plus up to an agreed to maximum amount. The owner and contractor share the risk. The owner is responsible up to the maximum price agreed to, and the contractor assumes responsibility for costs above that amount.

d. Cost-Plus Fixed Fee

The **cost-plus fixed fee** pricing method provides the owner some protection against the potential run-away expense of a cost-plus contract. The contractor agrees to be compensated for the cost of the project plus a fixed amount. While this eliminates the concern that the contractor will work to increase costs to increase profit, it also provides no incentive for the contractor to reduce costs

---

[7]   AIA A103–2007, art. 3 and § 7.1.1.

[8]   AIA A102–2007 5.2.1

because he will be paid the same fee regardless of the ultimate cost to the owner.

e. Unit Price

A contract (or part of a contract) may be priced on a **per-unit** (or fixed-unit) basis. With a unit price structure, the owner pays the contractor a set amount for each unit of material used on the project. For example, the owner may agree to pay a certain amount for each foot of pipe used or each linear foot of dirt removed from the job site.

It is not uncommon for fixed price contracts to have certain items that are not finalized or determined at the time the contractor is asked to submit a bid on the project. For those line items, the owner may ask the contractor to bid on a per unit basis based on an estimate of the number of units that will be needed. Such an approach provides the owner comparable bids to consider. Without such estimates, contractors would have an incentive to either pad their bid to address the uncertainty as to quantity of units or to reduce their bid to get the job and then seek an increase in the contract amount when the actual quantities are discovered.

Because unit prices are provided in the midst of some amount of uncertainty with regard to the ultimate amount of material that will be needed, there is a risk that the estimated amounts provided could be greatly off the mark—either significantly too high or too low. Dramatic variations from the estimate could place a significant burden on or give a windfall to the contractor. Absent a contractual provision to deal with significant variations, a court might require the contractor to perform, or might grant additional compensation, depending on how the court views the matter. In *Costanza Const. Corp. v. Rochester*, the contractor bid $25 per cubic yard to excavate rock on the site—which was below the actual cost to do the excavation. The specifications estimated 100 cubic yards of rock. The actual amount of rock was 600 cubic yards. The court refused to award additional compensation to the contractor—above the $25 per cubic yard bid—citing to the fact that the contractor contractually agreed to perform the work for that amount and that the owner disclaimed the accuracy of the estimate of the amount of rock.[9] Other courts have allowed the contractor additional compensation per unit, holding that the drastically increased number of units was unforeseen at the time the contract was entered into.[10] To deal with the issue up-front the parties may include a **variation in estimated quantity** clause in their contract. For example, the AIA contract provides that if the quantities are "materially changed" so that the unit price proposed would cause "substantial injury" to the contractor or owner, the per unit amount will be adjusted.[11]

---

[9] 537 N.Y.S.2d 394 (1989).

[10] Peter Kiewit Sons' Co. v. U.S., 74 F.Supp. 165 (Ct. Cl. 1947).

[11] AIA A201–2007 § 7.3.4. See FAR 52.211–18 (providing that if the actual quantity is more than 15% above or below the estimated quantity an adjustment to the contract price is appropriate).

6.   CONSTRUCTION FINANCING

Few owners can afford to finance a project out of their own pocket. All of the participants in a construction project rely on the owner to pay for the construction performed, and owner financial insecurity impacts all levels of the project. No one working on a construction project wants to find the owner is incapable of paying for work performed. To this end, the AIA documents provide that the contractor is entitled to evidence of the owner's ability to pay for the project before commencing construction.[12] After construction has commenced, if the owner fails to make payment, there is a change that will materially increase the amount due under the contract, or the contractor has evidence indicating the owner may be unable to make payments, the contractor can seek assurance of the owner's ability to pay. The contractor can suspend work until such proof is provided and if no assurance is forthcoming, the contractor can terminate the contract.[13]

Many owners fund a project with a **construction loan**. With a construction loan, the proceeds of the loan are used to complete the construction through "draws" from the loan balance. When construction is complete, the loan is paid back with funds from a traditional loan, with the bank taking a mortgage on the improved property to protect its investment. The financing entity's primary concerns are that the

---

[12]   AIA A201–2007 § 2.2.1.

[13]   AIA A201–2007 § 2.2.1 & § 14.1.1.4.

loan is paid back, and that its security interest in the property is protected. To satisfy the first interest the lender will seek to ensure that the owner will be able to make payments on the loan once the project is complete based on the owner's financial situation. The second concern arises if the owner does not use the loan money to make payments to the contractor or when contractors do not pay subcontractors, suppliers or other parties that might have the right to file a lien against the property that could be take priority over the lender's security interest.

The lender can address concerns about payment by including as a term of the loan that the owner have certification that work on the project has been done that coincides with the amount of the draw that the owner is seeking to take. Under the AIA documents, the architect makes precisely this certification when evaluating the contractor's payment application. The lender may also seek to protect itself by requiring lien waivers from those performing work on the project up to the amount of work performed.

B.   CONSTRUCTION PHASE OBLIGATIONS

1.   DUTY TO PROVIDE SITE ACCESS

The owner has an implied duty to ensure that those performing work on the project have physical access to the work site. While this implied obligation can be modified by contract, standard contracts place the obligation on the owner.[14] This means the

---

[14]   AIA A201–2007 § 2.2.2.

owner must obtain an easement if it is necessary for the contractor's material, equipment and/or employees to get to the site. It also means that an owner dealing with multiple prime contractors must ensure coordination, because issuing a notice to proceed to a contractor that cannot access the site because a prior contractor is still on site is a breach of the duty to provide site access. This obligation extends throughout the course of the project. Thus, where a storm downed trees and blocked a contractor's ability to get to the worksite, the owner was responsible for the delay due to the lack of access.[15]

The owner's obligation to ensure the right of access continues after performance has begun. There are a number of discoveries that could impact the ability of the contractor to move forward with construction that were not anticipated by or the fault of the contractor. For example, the contractor could discover protected wetlands or remains in unmarked graves. In these instances the contractor cannot continue (access to the site has been denied), and the owner has an obligation to remedy the problem. The AIA documents explicitly provide that the owner assumes responsibility to remedy the conditions to allow construction to continue.[16]

---

[15]   Northeast Clackamas County Electric Co-operative v. Continental Casualty Co., 221 F.2d 329 (9th Cir. 1955).

[16]   See AIA A201 § 3.7.5.

2. DUTY TO PROVIDE ACCURATE SITE INFORMATION

The owner has an implied duty to provide the contractor with complete and accurate information about conditions at the project site. If the owner is aware of adverse conditions and fails to inform the contractor, the owner can be liable to the contractor for the increased costs of carrying out the contract.

In the absence of some agreement up-front about what to do in the event that conditions on the construction site differ from what is expected, contractors would have an incentive to include a contingency amount in their contract to take into account the potential and in fact likelihood of unexpected conditions. This could greatly increase the cost to the owner. To address this issue, standardized contracts include a "differing site conditions" provision to address compensation when sites are different from what is usually found in the area. In addition, contractual provisions may also require the contractor to inspect the job site before bidding and take into account the visible condition of the property, and in those instances the contractor is responsible for what a reasonable inspection would have revealed.

3. DUTY TO PROVIDE ACCURATE DESIGN INFORMATION (*SPEARIN* DOCTRINE)

The owner has an implied obligation to ensure that the contractor receives accurate plans and specifications for a project, and the contractor has a right to rely on the design documents provided by the owner. The owner is responsible for the additional costs associated with the defective design. This is commonly referred to as the ***Spearin doctrine*** after the United States Supreme Court case *U.S. v. Spearin*, 248 U.S. 132 (1918). While the *Spearin* case itself applied only to federal contracts, almost all state courts have adopted the doctrine. The doctrine allows the contractor to rely on the design documents provided by the owner, and eliminates the need for a contractor to make costly determinations about the sufficiency of the design documents before bidding or increasing the bid to include a sufficient contingency to protect against defects in the design. Even if the owner hires a design professional to prepare the plans and specifications, the owner remains liable to the contractor for the actions of its agent-designer. When the designer and the contractor are contractually the same party—as in a design-build delivery system—the *Spearin* doctrine does not apply.

Contractors can use the *Spearin* doctrine as both a sword and a shield. If the owner asserts that the contractor's work is defective or that the contractor is liable for delay damages, the contractor can assert breach of the warranty as a defense. For example, where the design documents required a tunnel to be constructed using wood timbers, and the tunnel collapsed, the contractor was not liable to the owner for the cost of repair because the contractor acted in accordance with the plans.[17]

The contractor can also use the doctrine as a sword—by asserting a claim for increased cost or delays suffered as a result of the defective plans or specifications. Some courts have allowed the *Spearin* obligation to be expressly disclaimed in the contract. For example, a provision stating that the owner assumed no "responsibility for the data as being representative of the conditions and materials which may be encountered," was found to be sufficiently specific to deny the contractor's claim.[18] General provisions in the contract stating that the contractor has an obligation to examine the design documents or to inspect the project site are not sufficiently specific to work a disclaimer however.

There are some significant limitations on the *Spearin* doctrine. First, the doctrine applies to owner-directed **design specifications** and rarely to **performance specifications**. Design specifications dictate to the contractor exactly what material to use or how to perform, leaving no discretion. Performance specifications, on the other hand, dictate the results/performance required—but leave it up to the contractor how to achieve the required performance.

---

[17]   McConnell v. Corona City Water Co., 85 P. 929 (Cal. 1906).

[18]   McDevitt & Street Co. v. Marriott Corp., 713 F.Supp. 906, 911 (E.D. Va. 1989), *aff'd in part, rev'd in part on other grounds* 911 F.2d 723 (4th Cir. 1990).

Another limitation is that the defect must go to the essence of the project. If, overall the design is proper, the fact that the contractor has to request multiple clarifications of the design documents does not mean that the owner has violated the *Spearin* warranty. Third, the contractor's reliance on the plans and specifications must be reasonable. The contractor cannot follow plans that are patently and obviously incorrect and then shift liability to the owner. Fourth, the contractor must have complied with the plans and specifications as provided by the owner. If the contractor deviated from the plans provided, even though they are defective, *Spearin* is inapplicable. Finally, if the contract contains a "no-damage for delay" clause, the contractor will be entitled only to additional time to complete the project if the design documents are defective—and not damages.

CHAPTER 3

THE ROLE OF THE CONTRACTOR

A. INTRODUCTION

The contractor is responsible for constructing the project pursuant to the plans and specifications provided by the owner. Here, the word "contractor" refers to the **general contractor** or the party with the direct contractual relationship with the owner. How the owner selects the contractor depends on the nature of the project. Often on public projects the contractor must be selected through a public bidding process; however, in the private arena the owner is not limited to the bidding process.

B. CONTRACTING FOR A PROJECT

1. LICENSING REQUIREMENTS

Contractors seeking to bid on a project or enter into a construction contract, must be aware of the licensing requirements of the state where the construction will take place. Each state—and some local governments—have unique laws and regulations on what is required prior to entering into a construction contract. For example, Alabama requires out-of-state contractors to register with the Department of Revenue, provide a bond based on the amount of the contract, and provide a listing to the state of the equipment, etc. the contractor will use on the project.[1]

In addition to steps necessary to qualify to do work, states also require contractors to obtain a license in the state prior to entering into certain construction contracts. The purpose of these licensing requirements is to ensure those performing work in the state has a minimal amount of competence. Generally the licensing requirements include a written examination, fee, and bond. These licensing requirements are enforced by a regulatory body authorized to take disciplinary action against contractors that fail to abide by licensing laws. Apart from administrative discipline, failure to have a required license can have severe consequences, including disqualification from consideration for a project or, if awarded the contract, declaring the contract invalid. For example, Mississippi law declares any contract entered into in violation of the licensing laws "null and void."[2] Some states, such as California, even make failure to have a valid license a criminal offense.[3]

A contractor may expend the time and money preparing a bid only to have it rejected for failure to have a valid license. Even more consequential is when the contractor performs work on the contract and the owner refuses to pay because the contractor failed to have a valid license at the time the contract

---

[1]   Ala. Code Ann. § 39–2–14 (2014).

[2]   Miss. Code Ann. 31–3–15 (2014).

[3]   Cal. Bus. & Prof. Code § 7028 (2014).

was entered into. Courts will not enforce the contracts—which are declared illegal by statute. Such contractors are left in the unenviable position of either recovering nothing for the work performed or, more likely, having to rely on the doctrine of **quantum meruit**.

2.   BID MISTAKES

Contractors are often under a great deal of time pressure when preparing a bid to submit on a project. The frantic nature of the process can result in mistakes—whether the fault of the contractor or of a subcontractor submitting a quote to be included for a portion of the work. When this happens, the contractor will seek to revoke the offer, and if held to the contract could suffer great financial harm. However, often the bid documents will provide that, once a bid is open it is irrevocable. For example, in *Anco Construction Co. v. Witchita*, a contractor made a $95,000 error in their bid and sought to revoke it after the bids were opened and prior to being awarded the contract but the court refused— holding the contractor to its bid.[4] The rationale for this seeming harsh result is protection of the public bidding process. Courts reason that allowing a contractor to revoke a contract after learning that its bid was different from other bidders (even if drastically so) would allow contractors to manipulate the public bidding system.[5] In these

---

[4]   660 P.2d 560 (Kan. 1983).

[5]   White Hat Management LLC v. Ohio Farmers Ins. Co., 856 N.E. 2d 991, 997 (Ct. App. Ohio 2006).

situations, if the contractor cannot afford to enter into the contract and absorb the loss it will be forced instead to forfeit the bid bond if one is required on the project. Most courts, however, applying the doctrine of **unilateral mistake** will allow the contractor to revoke a bid under certain conditions. It should be noted that a subcontractor who makes a mistake in calculating its bid may assert the right of recission against the contractor on the same basis as the contractor asserting the right against the owner.

The first thing to note is what a mistake is *not*—it is not a mistake of judgment. In other words, if the contractor consciously included an amount in a bid and subsequently learns that its bid is lower than other bidders, courts will hold that this was a business decision, a mistake in judgment—and the law will not allow the contractor to rescind the contract. A mistake that may allow a contractor to escape performance must be one of fact. Examples of the factual mistakes that may justify recission include "faulty addition, omission of items, typographical errors, misplaced decimals, errors in transferring items from detailed summary sheets, transposition of numbers, [and] misinterpretation of specifications. . . ."[6] Rescission for mistake is an equitable doctrine and courts will look at the underlying facts to determine whether the contract should be enforced. Factors courts will consider are: (1) whether it would be unconscionable to hold the contractor to the contract; (2) whether the mistake goes to the fundamental consideration (money in the

---

6   Bruner & O'Connor on Construction Law § 2:119.

construction context) of the contract; (3) whether the mistake occurred despite the diligence of the contractor; and (4) whether it would be possible to place the owner in the position they were in before.[7]

The case of *M.J. McGough Co. v. Jane Lamb Memorial Hospital* provides a good sense of how the bidding process works and how courts apply the doctrine of mistake.[8] The owner, a hospital, sought bids for renovations. The bids were due on February 16th, and M.J. McGough Co. was accepting bids from various subcontractors for portions of the work right up until the deadline—the court notes that it is customary for subcontractors to wait until the last minute to submit bids (this is a strategic action to prevent the contractor from having time to use the subcontractor's bid to leverage a lower quote from another subcontract). Mr. McGough received a telephone call from Artcraft Interiors whose quote was $222,000. Mr. McGough wrote down the quote and then verbally told an employee the quote amount, but instead of writing the correct amount the employee entered $22,2000 into the bid sheet and this amount was included in the bid. The court noted that this was a clerical error, the contractor acted quickly to withdraw the bid and to enforce it would be unconscionable. Therefore, the court allowed recission of the contract based on mistake.

---

[7]   Kenneth E. Curran, Inc. v. State, 215 A.2d 702, 703–04 (N.H. 1965).

[8]   302 F.Supp. 482 (S.D. Iowa 1969).

C.   CONSTRUCTION AND TIME

Time is of the essence in the construction industry. Time is money and a delayed project can result in the owner losing a great deal of revenue or at the very least the ability to use the project as anticipated and a contractor being forced to forego another project or incur increased labor or material costs. While historically construction contracts (as well as other contracts involving real estate) were viewed as subject to too much uncertain to bind a party to performance by a certain date, with modern technology and scheduling software, this has changed and is reflected in the fact that standard contracts now explicitly include a time is of the essence clause.[9] By including this provision, the parties are recognizing that failure to finish by the agreed upon date is a breach of contract. Typically the contractor agrees to commence work upon receiving a **notice to proceed** from the owner, and agrees to have the work completed either by a certain date or by a number of days after issuance of the notice to proceed.[10] Of course, if the contract does not include a time is of the essence clause, the common rule of completion within a reasonable time is implied into the contract.

While including a time is of the essence clause makes the completion date an enforceable contractual obligation, just like other contractual obligations, the completion date can be waived by

---

9   AIA A201–2007 § 8.2.1.

10   AIA A101–2007 § 3.1.

the actions of the party. For example, if the owner continues to issue change orders on the project after the established completion date and accept/pay for the contractor's work the owner has likely waived the right to assert that the contractor's failure to complete the project by the contract date was a material breach. If the owner is willing to continue with the project after the established completion date, courts imply that the owner no longer considers time of the essence. If a waiver is found, the owner is not entitled to damages (liquidated or otherwise) for late completion. If the completion date is waived courts hold that the contractor must complete the project within a reasonable time. The traditional rule is that the owner may unilaterally set a new date for completion, but the date must provide a reasonable amount of time to complete the project based on the circumstances.

D.   DUTY TO COORDINATE WORK: SCHEDULING AND DELAY

The contractor can enter into a contract with a firm completion date because scheduling methods are so advanced. A common approach for developing a schedule for a project is known as the **critical path method**. This approach requires the contractor to create a chronological schedule for the portions for work to be performed on the project. Each portion is given an estimated time for start and completion. For most activities there is some amount of float incorporated into the schedule. This means that there is some slack in the schedule where delay of a particular portion of work will not delay the entire project. However, there are also portions of the project that are considered on the critical path and if those portions of work are delayed, then it will impact the completion date. As the project progresses, the contractor is able to enter any unanticipated delays into the program and see the impact on the project. Subcontractors, who are directly impacted by how the work is scheduled are typically not consulted in preparation of the schedule. However, the ConsensusDOCS (unlike the AIA documents), explicitly contemplates scheduling coordination between the contractor and subcontractor.[11]

Even the best laid schedule can run into unforeseen events. When this happens, the project completion date may be pushed beyond what was agreed to in the contract. Identifying responsibility for the delay is crucial on a construction project. A contractor will be entitled to additional compensation or more time to complete the project if the delays are attributable to the owner or design professional. On the other hand, if the contractor (or subcontractors) are responsible for the delay, for example when the contractor fails to adequately schedule, sequence or coordinate construction, the owner may be entitled to charge the contractor liquidated damages or seek direct (and possibly consequential) damages from the contractor.

---

[11]   ConsensusDocs 750 § 5.2.

1. DELAY CLAIMS

a. "Excusable" and "Nonexcusable" Delays

Whether a contractor is entitled to money damages or more time for a delay in project completion will depend on the reason for the delay. Delays on a project can occur for innumerable reasons—some the fault of the various parties and some the result of natural occurrences. Standard contracts typically break down delays into excusable and nonexcusable.

i. Excusable Delays

Excusable delays are those which are not the responsibility of the contractor. These types of delays can be divided into two types: **uncompensable excusable delay** or **compensable excusable delay**.

An excusable but uncompensable delay is one in which no parties to the contract are responsible. For example, acts of God or strikes which delays the project completion date are excusable but will not entitle the contractor to compensation for costs incurred as a result of the delay. However, the contractor is entitled to additional time beyond the established completion date to complete the project without being in breach of contract.[12] An excusable delay must also be unforeseeable. Therefore, a contractor cannot claim weather delays as constituting an excusable delay when the project

---

[12]   See AIA A201–2007 § 8.3.1.

only experienced normal weather conditions; however, if the contractor can demonstrate that the weather was abnormally bad, the contractor may be able to classify it as an excusable delay.

Excusable and compensable delays are delays caused by the owner or the owner's agent (usually the design professional) which impact the critical path and therefore the ultimate completion date. Delays that merely cause changes in the schedule of the trades are not compensable unless they impact the final completion date. Examples of conduct that could delay the project are numerous and include failure to provide timely access to the project site, the failure to timely review and respond to requests for clarification regarding the plans or specifications, overzealous inspections that interfere with construction, and issuance of an excessive number of change orders. If the contractor suffers delays that are compensable, and the contract does not contain a provision limiting the contractor's right to recover monetary damages, the contractor is entitled both to an extension of time to complete the project as well as the costs incurred as a result of the delay. These costs may include the increase in labor or material, the increase in the cost of performing work (perhaps because the project has been pushed into poor weather conditions), and the increased share of administrative costs—such as home office overhead that must be devoted to the project. A common formula used to calculate the amount of overhead that can appropriately assigned to the delay on a particular project is known as the

***Eichleay* formula.**[13] The formula, developed in a government contracting case, has been accepted by a number of state courts as a mechanism to calculate overhead delay damages. A contractor can also recover for profit lost as a result of the delay. These same concepts apply to subcontractors as well. For example, if the contractor fails to properly schedule or coordinate with the various trades on a project and the subcontractor is delayed in completing its scope of work, the subcontractor has suffered an excusable and compensable delay.

ii. Non-Excusable Delay

Absent a contractual or legal justification for delaying completion, the contractor assumes the risk that she will not be able to complete the project in a timely manner. Therefore, delays in completion which are not categorized as excusable are non-excusable. The contractor is also responsible for delay caused by those the contractor is responsible for—including subcontractors and suppliers. A contractor is not entitled to compensation in these situations and may be charged with the damages suffered by the owner as a result of the delay in completion.

b. No Damage for Delay Clause

To limit liability, prime contracts and subcontracts (either explicitly or through flow down provisions) include **no damage for delay** provisions. These clauses provide that, no matter

---

[13]   In re Eichleay Corp., ASBCA No. 5183, 60–2 BCA (1960).

what the basis or cause of a delay, the contractor/subcontractor is not entitled to damages. Instead, the sole remedy is a request for additional time. Courts generally enforce these provisions. However, courts have refused to limit the contractor's recover when: (1) the delay is so long it constitutes an abandonment; (2) delay was caused by fraud, misrepresentation, or concealment; and (3) where the delays are the result of active interference.[14] It is important to note that neither the AIA form documents nor the ConsensusDocs contain a no damage for delay clause. However, the AIA reciprocal waiver of consequential damages provision may drastically limit the right to recover even without an express no damage for delay clause.

c. Concurrent Delays

Events that delay project completion beyond the contractual completion date may not be solely attributed to either the owner or the contractor, but instead be the result of the actions of both. These are known as **concurrent delays**. Courts are split on how to address concurrent delays. Historically, courts would deny both parties the right to claim any damages as a result of the delay and merely grant the contractor additional time to finish the project. This has significant impacts on all involved. The owner is denied the right to assess liquidated damages and the contractor is denied the right to assess costs incurred as a result of the delay. The

---

[14]   J.A. Jones Const. Co. v. Lehrer McGovern Bovis, Inc., 89 P.3d 1009, 1016 (Nev. 2004).

minority position (but with growing support) is to apportion liability and allow recovery based on percentage of responsibility.[15]

d. Acceleration of Work

Another issue in the delay context is acceleration of work. **Acceleration** comes in two forms. First is a demand by the owner that the contractor accelerate the speed of construction and finish prior to the agreed-to date of completion in the contract. Second is commonly known as **constructive acceleration** where the owner refuses to grant the contractor additional time to complete the project despite excusable/compensable delays, requiring the contractor to increase the pace of construction to make up for previous delays on the project and meet the contractual completion date. Acceleration of work increases the cost to the contractor—including the cost of additional manpower, payment of overtime, and rental of additional equipment. In both of these situations, if the contractor can establish its right to additional time/compensation under the contract—that is, demand and denial for additional time, the presence of a compensable/excusable delay, and evidence that the delay would ultimately impact the completion date—the contractor can recover its costs.

For example, in *Sherman R. Smoot Co. v. Ohio Dep't of Admin. Services*, the contractor argued that the owner improperly rejected his claims for an

---

[15]   Bruner & O'Connor on Construction Law § 7:195.

extension of time for 47 days due to an excusable delay—abnormal weather conditions.[16] The contractor sought the costs he incurred in having to accelerate as a result of the rejection of the claim. The court first noted that if the contractor could establish his claim for constructive acceleration he would be able to recover his increased costs to complete before the completion date. On the facts, however, the court held that the contractor could not establish that the delay due to weather was excusable because the weather events were not abnormal. Because the contractor could not establish a wrongfully rejected request for additional time, the contractor was not entitled to recoup the costs for doing what the contractor agreed to do in the contract—complete the project by the contract date.

E. PROJECT SAFETY

Construction is one of the most dangerous occupations in the United States. Concerns over workplace safety and compensation for workplace injuries are persistent. Regulations addressing safety on the project occur at the federal, state, and local level. The federal agency is the **Occupational Safety & Health Administration ("OSHA")** and states have equivalent regulatory bodies. OSHA regulations seek to ensure that employees on a job site avoid known health and safety hazards, and place the obligation on the employer to meet this standard. Examples of the types of conduct OSHA

---

[16]   736 N.E.2d 69, 78 (Ct. App. Ohio 2000).

regulates includes the use of safety equipment, prevention of exposure to harmful chemicals, and exposure to unguarded dangerous machines.

Injuries on the worksite are inevitable, and compensation for those injuries is provided through the state-administered **workers' compensation** regulatory scheme if the injured worker is categorized as an employee. The workers' compensation program is meant to provide certain payment to employees injured in the course and scope of employment by requiring employers to pay compensation regardless of the employee's fault. On the other hand, the employee gives up the possibility for a larger amount of damages for the certainty of payment that is not reduced by comparative fault.

Often workers/employees of a subcontractor will seek compensation beyond what is provided by the workers' compensation scheme. Perhaps the subcontractor employer does not carry workers' compensation insurance or the injured worker does not feel the amount recovered under the workers' compensation scheme is sufficient compensation for the nature of the injury. These individuals often seek compensation from others on the job site— including contractors and design professionals. The general rule is that contractors/design professionals are not liable for injuries to independent contractors such as the workers on the job site not employed by the contractor or design professional. However, this rule has a number of exceptions that can lead to liability in particular cases. By far the most common situation where courts impose liability is where the contractor/design professional assumed responsibility (either by contract or in fact) for work site safety and performed that obligation negligently.

F.   PAYMENT FOR WORK PERFORMED

The method and procedure for payment by the owner will be set out in the construction contract. While there is no required procedure, the standard contracts adopt a process whereby a contractor submits a periodic (often monthly) **application for payment** to the owner. The request for payment reflects the amount of work performed since the last payment request. A common way for a contractor to present the amount of work done (and left to do) on a payment application is by including a **schedule of values**. A schedule of values is a listing of each element of work with a value—dollar amount—on the work. Then, the payment application reflects the percentage of the particular scope of work done since the last pay period and that amount is deducted from the total amount due for the portion of work. Once the portion of work is complete, the amount completed is 100% and the contract amount remaining to be paid is zero dollars.

If the owner is satisfied that the work reflected in the application was actually performed and performed in accordance with the contract documents, the owner issues payment for that portion of the work. These types of periodic payments are commonly called **progress**

payments. Of course, it may be very difficult for the owner to know if the contractor has performed the work and/or performed it in accordance with the contract documents. Therefore, the standard contracts provide that the owner can rely on the design professional to evaluate the payment application and certify that the identified work either has or has not been completed in accordance with the contract documents.

Owners are concerned that contractors will have no incentive to finish the project if they receive full payment throughout the project because as the project is moves toward completion there will be less and less left of the contract amount. To avoid this, and to ensure that the owner has a fund in the event the contractor's work is defective, the owner will hold back a percentage of the amount due to the contractor. This is called **retainage**. Typically the percentage retained is from 5 to 10 percent of the progress payment amount. Most of this retainage is returned to the contractor upon substantial completion and the remainder is returned upon final completion. Retainage can put the contractor in financial difficulties because the contractor has to pay subcontractors and suppliers for work performed, and does not have the amounts retained by the owner to make those payments. To address this concern some states have enacted laws that govern retainage—for example by reducing the amount of retainage as construction proceeds or by requiring the owner to place retainage in an interest bearing escrow account.

G.   SUBSTANTIAL COMPLETION

If the contract sets out a completion date or time frame for construction, the obligation to complete the project by the agreed-to date is satisfied if the project reaches the level of **substantial completion**. Substantial completion is considered "that point in the construction where the work is sufficiently complete that the owner may occupy or utilize the work for the use for which it was intended."[17] The AIA documents adopt this standard.[18] The architect is charged with certifying to the owner that the project is substantially complete under the AIA documents.[19] Generally when a certificate of occupancy is issued on a project it is at the point of substantial completion.

Substantial completion does not mean that the project is complete or that all work is finished. In fact, it is anticipated that there will be minor issues that remain to be addressed—known as **punchlist items**. To ensure that the contractor completes the punchlist items, the owner has the right to retain enough money to cover the cost of the remaining items.[20] The EJCDC documents contemplate the owner retaining up to 200 percent of the cost of the outstanding items.[21]

---

[17]   Bruner & O'Connor on Construction Law § 8:23.

[18]   AIA A201–2007 § 9.8.1.

[19]   AIA A201–2007 § 9.8.3.

[20]   AIA A201–2007 § 9.8.5.

[21]   EJCDC C–520 § 6.02(B).

Substantial completion is such an important concept in the construction arena because it has significant consequences. First, responsibility for the structure is turned over to the owner. Second, the contractor is entitled to all retainage held by the owner except for that amount necessary to complete punchlist items. Third, the contractor cannot be terminated for default—the owner is limited to recovering the cost to address the punchlist items. Fourth, the owner liquidated damages charges terminate. Finally, the contractual warranty period commences.

H.   FINAL COMPLETION

When a project reaches **final completion**, all work, including the punchlist items, is complete and all paperwork (operating manuals, warranty documents) has been turned over to the owner. The architect, under the AIA documents, will issue a final certificate of payment, recommending that the owner release all remaining amounts due to the contractor.[22] Final completion and payment also constitutes a waiver of claims by the owner against the contractor for construction except those expressly excluded—including unsettled lien claims, failure of the work to comply with the contract documents, and warranty claims.[23] Thus, the owner is not waiving the right to claim that work—no matter when completed—does not conform to the contract documents. Certainly the owner is not

---

[22]   AIA A201 § 9.10.

[23]   AIA A201 § 9.10.4.

accepting latent defects; however, an owner may have waived claims with regard to patent defects. Upon acceptance of final payment, the contractor waives all claims against the owner except those made in writing and pending at the time of final payment.[24]

I.   TERMINATION

When the contractor and owner first enter into a contract, they both hope that the project will be completed on time, within budget, and without dispute. The reality is, however, that sometimes either the owner or the contractor or both will seek to terminate the contract before the project is complete. This section discusses when termination is available to the parties and the consequences of wrongful termination. If the parties mutually agree to terminate (**rescind**) the contract the parties are only entitled to damages as set out in the rescission agreement and both parties walk away from the contract. Disputes arise, however, when one party attempts to unilaterally terminate the contract.

1.   TERMINATION UNDER THE COMMON LAW

If there is no provision in the contract setting out the justifications and process for termination, then the common law standard for termination— **material breach**—is applied. If a breach is not material, the non-breaching party is entitled to

---

[24]   AIA A201 § 9.10.5.

damages but does not have a right to terminate the contract. Identifying a breach as material is fact-dependent. The Restatement (Second) of Contracts provides five factors to consider when evaluating the significance of the breach: (a) whether the injured party will be deprived a benefit that was expected; (b) whether the injured party can be compensated for the benefit not received; (c) the extent to which the breaching party will suffer a forfeiture; (d) the likelihood of curing the breach; and (e) whether the breaching party acted in good faith.[25] If either the contractor or owner commits a material breach of the contract then the other party is excused from performing and can recover the damages suffered as a result of the breach. For example, if the contractor abandons the project without justification, the owner can recover the cost to finish the project. Declaring a party in material breach is risky, however. If it is subsequently determined that the breach was not sufficiently serious to constitute a material breach, the party that terminated the contract could be liable for a material breach for wrongful termination.

Standard contracts contain explicit contractual bases for termination. The contractual provisions provide situations where the contractor or owner can terminate the contract **for cause** (for a material breach) and the owner can terminate **for convenience**. By adopting these contractually agreed to bases for termination, the parties have the certainty of knowing that the right to terminate the

---

[25]   § 241.

contract will be limited to the situations set out in the contract. It is important to note, however, that the party seeking to terminate a contract for cause still has the burden of demonstrating that the other party's breach was material or risk a finding of wrongful termination

2.   OWNER TERMINATION OF CONTRACTOR FOR CAUSE

Standardized contracts set out specific circumstances where the owner can terminate the contractor for cause. In the construction industry when an owner terminates a contractor for cause it is often said that the contractor is in **default**. AIA A201–2007 § 14.2.1 through 14.2.4 provides that the owner can terminate the contractor for cause if: (a) the contractor "repeatedly fails to supply enough properly skilled workers or proper materials"; (b) fails to pay subcontractors; (c) repeatedly disregards laws, regulations or orders of a public body; or (d) is responsible for a "substantial breach" of other contractual provisions. If the project has reached substantial completion then by definition the project is to the point that it is capable of being occupied by the owner and therefore, any breach by the contractor after substantial completion is not considered material, and the owner is limited to recover costs incurred to remedy the defect. The requirement that the contractor *repeatedly* fail to supply enough workers/material for the project or disregard laws is no accident. This language is to make it clear that the contractor has more than minor (non-material) worker shortages or law violations—but instead that the actions are substantial and often enough to constitute a material breach of the contract. The AIA documents have the unique requirement that the initial decision maker certify that the there is sufficient justification before the contractor can be terminated.[26]

If an owner terminates a contractor for cause, courts often imply into the contract the requirement that the owner provide the contractor an opportunity to cure the default. Standardized contracts often address this issue directly by requiring a certain amount of notice prior to termination. The AIA contract requires seven days' notice both the contractor and the contractor's surety if the job is bonded.[27] There is some dispute over the purpose of the time between the notice and the termination. One position is that the time is intended to give the contractor an opportunity to cure the default during this time frame. Others argue that the time between notice and termination is intended merely to give the contractor an opportunity to remove all equipment and materials from the job site. The third interpretation is that the time period is to give the parties an opportunity to consider the consequences of termination (and perhaps whether there is really evidence of a material breach) and decide whether to go through with the termination.

---

[26]   AIA A201–2007 § 14.2.2.

[27]   AIA A201–2007 § 14.2.2.

If the contractor has performed work and has not received payment at the time of termination, the owner is entitled to retain those amounts and to use them to off-set the cost of the owner to finish the project. If, after completion, there are funds remaining that are due to the contractor, then the owner must turn those amounts over to the contractor. The likelihood of there being money remaining due after default, however, is not great. In fact, what is more likely is that completion of the contract will cost the owner more than is owed to the contractor and in that situation the owner is entitled to recover these additional amounts from the contractor.

An owner that terminates a construction contract still wants to have the project completed with as little disruption as possible. To facilitate this the AIA contract provides the owner has several rights regarding the project when the contractor is terminated for cause. First is the right of the owner to take possession of equipment, materials, and other items belonging to the contractor that are left on the project site.[28] The owner may also accept assignment of the subcontracts entered into by the contractor—although the owner does not have to.[29] Finally, the owner has the right to finish the work and the contractor has the right to an accounting of the costs incurred by the owner in finishing the project.[30] While it may seem obvious that the owner

---

[28]   AIA A201–2007 § 14.2.2.1.

[29]   AIA A201–2007 § 14.2.2.2.

[30]   AIA A201–2007 § 14.2.2.3.

has the right to continue construction after default, without this express provision the contractor could argue that the project must wait until contractor disputes over the appropriateness of the termination—that is that the termination was wrongful—prior to the owner recommencing work. Pursuant to this provision the owner can continue working on the project despite outstanding disputes.

3. OWNER TERMINATION OF CONTRACTOR FOR CONVENIENCE

There is no common law right to terminate for convenience or without cause. At common law, the termination of a contract without the presence of a material breach was wrongful and entitled the non-breaching party to damages. Therefore, when a construction contract includes a provision allowing termination for convenience it is in contravention to the common law and is interpreted narrowly. AIA A201–2007 § 14.4.1 provides that the owner may at any time terminate the contract for any reason (the contractor does not have the right to terminate for convenience). If the owner exercises its right to terminate for convenience, the contractor is obligated to cease work, demobilize equipment, and terminate any contracts entered into with regard to the project.[31] If the owner terminates for convenience the contractor is entitled to payment (including overhead and profit) for work completed prior to the termination, costs incurred as a result of the termination, and overhead and profit for the

---

[31]   AIA A201–2007 § 14.4.2.1–.3.

part of the project not completed. This is one of the rare situations where the contractor is entitled to profit for work not performed.[32]

4.   CONTRACTOR TERMINATION FOR CAUSE

The reasons a contractor can terminate for cause are more limited than those of the owner. There are two reasons that the contractor's right to terminate is limited. First is because when disputes arise between owner and contractor, the contractor is contractually obligated to continue working on the project and to subsequently go through the dispute process. This limitation essentially means that all disputes regarding changes and scope of work are resolved through the claims process and not by declaring the owner in default. Second, the contractual bases for terminating are also limited. AIA A201–2007 provides that the contractor can terminate for cause if work is stopped for thirty consecutive days because: (a) a public authority issues an order stopping work; (b) an action by the government such as the declaration of a national emergency that causes work to be stopped; (c) the architect has failed to certify payment or the owner has failed to make payment as contemplated by the contract; or (d) the owner fails to provide sufficient evidence of owner financial viability when required.[33] The contractor can terminate only when these events occur "through no act or fault of the Contractor" or a party the contractor is responsible

---

[32]   AIA A201–2007 § 14.4.3.

[33]   AIA A201–2007 § 14.1.1.1–.4.

for.[34] Therefore, if the contractor bears any fault for the owner's actions the contractor is not entitled to terminate for cause. The contractor must also give the owner notice seven days before terminating the contract.[35]

What this means in practice is that the contractor's primary basis for termination for cause is the owner's failure to pay. However, even this right is limited because the termination for cause provision contemplates termination when the owner fails to pay the amounts certified as due under the contract. Therefore, if the contractor disputes the amount that the architect certifies, the contractor's only remedy is to resolve the disputes through the procedures set out in the contract (mediation, arbitration, or litigation). Add to this the fact that the contractor must continue to work during the course of these disputes and the limitation on the contractor's right to terminate for cause becomes clear.

If the contractor properly terminates the contract for cause, the contractor is entitled to recover for the work the contractor completed prior to termination—including an amount for overhead and profit. The contractor can also recover costs incurred as a result of the termination and damages.[36]

---

[34]   AIA A201–2007 § 14.1.1.

[35]   AIA A201–2007 § 14.1.3.

[36]   AIA A201–2007 § 14.1.3.

5.   WRONGFUL TERMINATION

Declaring a party in default and terminating the contract carries risks. The foremost risk is that a court or arbitrator analyzing the circumstances surrounding the termination will determine that there was not a sufficient basis for terminating the contract. This could be because the underlying basis asserted for termination could not be established or because there a determination that any breach that occurred was not material. There could also be a finding that the party terminating the contract waived the basis for termination, and was not entitled to use the action to justify termination.

A contractor wrongfully declared in default is entitled to its expectation damages. This would include all amounts currently due to the contractor at the time of termination as well as lost profit for the work not performed. The contractor is also entitled to the direct costs related to the termination—including the costs of demobilization and any amounts the contractor has to pay to subcontractors/suppliers as a result of the termination. If consequential damages have not been waived in the contract, the contractor would also be entitled to foreseeable consequential damages.

When a contractor walks away from a project wrongfully declaring the owner in default, the owner is entitled to the cost incurred in completing work on the project. The contractor is liable for the entire amount despite the fact that it will almost always be more than the amount remaining due under the terminated contract.

CHAPTER 4

THE ROLE OF THE DESIGN PROFESSIONAL

A. INTRODUCTION

The desire of the owner dictates the design of a project. The design professional works with the owner to develop a project design that satisfies the owner's aesthetic, functional, and budget goals. Whether the design professional on a project is an architect or an engineer depends on the type of project being built. An architect is typically retained on buildings that will ultimately be occupied while engineers may be the lead design professional on projects where the primary emphasis is on functionality—for example civil construction projects such as bridges or treatment plants.

The relationship between the owner and the design professional is established by contract and common law obligations. The contract sets out the **basic services** that the design professional will provide.[1] It is important that the owner know precisely what the design professional is contractually obligated to do because any services sought beyond the basic services are considered **additional services** and will increase the contract price.

---

[1] AIA Doc. B101–2007 Article 3; EJCDC E–500 § 3.2 (2008); ConsensusDOCS 240 Art. 1.

In addition to contractual obligations, as professionals, design professionals must perform with a minimum amount of competence in their field, and if they fall below this standard they can subject to a tort claim for breach of professional standard of care as well as breach of contract. The extent of involvement the design professional will have in the construction phase of the project depends on the needs of the owner. The AIA documents contemplate that the design professional will remain the owner's agent throughout the construction process. Practically this makes sense because the design documents as contemplated on the drafting table inevitably will change/need clarification when the construction phase begins. However, if the owner's needs are merely design related, the parties can agree that the design professional's services will be limited to the design documents.

B.   COMMON CONTRACTUAL PROVISIONS IN THE DESIGN PHASE

There are several common contractual provisions setting out the obligations of the owner and design professional in the design (pre-construction) phase. The goal of these provisions is to make sure that all parties are aware of precisely what the design professional is agreeing to do and to keep the owner informed and satisfied as the design moves toward finalization. The design professional is concerned that the owner will seek to drastically change the nature of the design as the process commences and then expect the design professional to modify the design at no cost. Notice how the procedures set out, which are similar in major standardized contracts, seek to address this by requiring owner approval at each stage of the design process.[2]

1.   DESIGN SERVICES

The first responsibility of a design professional is to design a project consistent with the owner's goals. In creating the design the relationship between the owner and designer is that of independent contractor. Identifying the nature of the relationship is important because the designer can wear three different hats throughout the construction process, with each imposing differing legal obligations. In addition to acting as an independent contractor, the designer may also act as the owner's agent and as a neutral decision-maker during the construction phase of the project. As an independent contractor, the designer will prepare the design documents consistent with the competence required in their industry—and can refuse to incorporate aspects into the design that would violate those professional obligations even if the owner insists. If the designer fails to meet the minimum level of competence required by their profession, third parties with no contractual relationship with the design professional can bring a tort claim for negligence in preparation of the design or negligent misrepresentation based on statements made in the

---

[2]   These are the general procedures set out in both the AIA and ConsensusDOCS.

design documents if they are injured as a result of the defect.

a. Schematic Design Phase

The owner and design professional must meet and determine the owner's objectives, budget, and priorities for the project. These elements constitute the project **program** which the owner has an obligation to provide and which guides the design professional in preparation of design documents. Using the information developed in discussions with the owner, the designer develops a **preliminary design** for the project, which incorporates the "scale and relationship" of the project.[3] Once the owner approves the preliminary design, the designer prepares the **schematic design documents**. The design at this point includes an estimate of project cost and takes into account jurisdictional requirements for the structure such as zoning and includes a general layout of the floor plan and spatial aspects of the project. Before moving to the next phase the designer must obtain the owner's approval of the schematic design.

b. Design Development Phase

Once the owner has approved the schematic design documents, the design professional prepares the **design development documents**. These documents are further revisions of the design. While still not detailed enough to build from, the design now includes the layout of the electrical,

---

[3]   AIA B101–2007 § 3.2.4.

mechanical, and structural features of the project. The documents likely also include location of features such as doors and windows. The design professional does not move forward to the next phase until receiving owner approval of the documents.

c. Construction Document Phase

Once the owner has approved the Design Development documents, the design professional prepares the **construction documents**. These are the plans and specifications the contractor will rely on to build the structure. These are the documents provided to bidders to prepare their bid if the project is put out for bid.

The key here is that the design process progresses in steps, with the design professional and owner communicating and cooperating at each step of the process. It may be that, because of the nature of the project, all of these steps are not necessary. For example, the EJCDC contract contemplates an initial **Report** setting out the basic schematics of the project, a preliminary design phase and then a final design phase.[4]

2.   BIDDING AND NEGOTIATION SERVICES

It is common for a design professional, once the construction documents are prepared, to assist the owner in putting the project out for bid and

---

[4]   EJCDC E–500 § A1.01–A1.03 (2008); ConsensusDOCS 240 § 2.1.

selecting a contractor. For example, in the AIA documents, the architect assists the owner in the administration of the bidding process—making copies and distributing bidding documents to prospective bidders, and conducting the opening of bids. The architect also has substantive responsibilities—holding a pre-bid conference and responding to questions from prospective bidders about the bid documents.[5]

3.   CONSTRUCTION SERVICES

While the administrative responsibilities a design professional may assume during construction are discussed in detail later, it is important to note that the relationship between the design professional and the owner shifts from the design phase to the construction services phase. While preparing design documents the design professional maintains her professional independence from the owner, and acts as an independent contractor. However, during the construction phase, the designer acts as the agent of her principal the owner. That shift in relationship means that the design professional assumes certain duties and responsibilities to the owner, and must act at the direction of the owner.

C.   DESIGNING TO A BUDGET

A fundamental element of the design from the perspective of the owner which can lead to disputes is project cost. The design goals of the owner and the

---

[5]   AIA B101–2007 § 3.5.2.2.

cost to achieve those goals may not align. The design professional may believe that any cost estimate provided is little more than an educated guess while the owner may seek to hold the designer to the estimate. The goal is to ensure there is a clear line of communication between the parties so that both sides understand their obligations. One of the worst things that can happen is a design that does not fit within the owner's budget—and therefore either cannot be constructed or costs the owner much more than budgeted. To avoid disputes, standard contracts provide a number of provisions that address designing within a budget. These provisions do not make the design professional guarantor of the budget's cost, but ensure that at every step of the process the design professional and owner are communicating about budget issues. It should be noted that if the design professional's failure to have a realistic budget falls below what a minimally competent professional would provide, then the design professional could be liable in malpractice for tort damages for negligent estimating.[6]

While standard contracts seek to ensure that the design professional is not the guarantor of cost, if a guaranteed maximum price is included in the contract, the architect will be held responsible if she fails to design the project within budget. In addition, some courts have held that contract language stating that the design professional "does not guarantee" the cost estimates is a statement that

---

[6]   Kellogg v. Pizza Oven, Inc., 402 P.2d 633 (Colo. 1965).

the design professional cannot exactly anticipate the cost, but imposes an obligation on the designer to accurately provide a "reasonable approximation" of the cost.[7] To avoid potential designer liability, the AIA documents specifically provide that if the project comes in above budget, the owner has several options: increasing the budget, put the project out for rebidding, work with the architect to reduce the cost of the work (and the architect agrees to modify the design for no additional compensation), or terminate the contract with the architect.[8]

There is a split of authority on when a designer who assumes an obligation to design to a budget breaches the obligation. A minority of courts say that if the designer misses the budget mark at all the designer has breached the contract, while the majority, recognizing the uncertainties in the construction industry, will find a breach only where the difference between the budget and ultimate cost is substantial. If there is a finding that the design professional assumed an obligation to design to a particular budget and breaches that obligation, the owner is entitled to recover fees paid to the designer. The owner may also be entitled to the difference between the estimated cost and actual cost of construction (although some jurisdictions will reduce this difference to accommodate for overruns that would be expected on any project). The owner

---

[7]   Durand Associates v. Guardian Inv. Co., 183 N.W.2d 246, 250 (Neb. 1971).

[8]   AIA B101–2007 §§ 6.6, 6.7.

may also be entitled to consequential damages as a result of the breach—unless that category have been waived by contract.

D.   DESIGNING "GREEN" BUILDINGS

There is a movement to emphasize energy efficient building design and construction. Green buildings can benefit not only the environment, but also the owner of the project through a savings in the cost of energy as well as incentives provided by the government. However, as with any new and developing area, the legal issues that will arise with green construction are in their infancy. This section first introduces the concept of green building design.

The EPA defines a green building as a structure built "using processes that are environmentally responsible and resource-efficient throughout a building's life-cycle from siting [where to build a structure] to design, construction, operation, maintenance, renovation and deconstruction."[9] Thus, defining a building as "green" takes into consideration much more than just the building materials used or the design features incorporated into the structure. Considerations include: (a) the efficient use of energy, water, and other resources; (b) protection of the health of occupants; and (c) the impact of the building on the environment—including siting issues and waste production.

Buildings may be built and designed to take into account environmental concerns, or existing

---

[9]   http://www.epa.gov/greenbuilding/pubs/about.htm.

buildings can be **retrofitted** to make them more environmentally friendly. There are a number of standards used to identify and label how "green" a building is. The most commonly used are the **Leadership in Energy and Environmental Design (LEED)** standards drafted by the U.S. Green Building Council in 1998. A building that meets the LEED criteria can receive certification in one of four categories: certified, silver, gold, and platinum. Other ratings systems include the EPA **Energy Star** program, the Green Building Initiative's **Green Globes** program. In addition to these third-party programs, federal, state and local governments have also enacted laws and ordinances either mandating or incentivizing environmentally friendly construction.

LEED is the most common and popular standards in the U.S. While LEED standards were developed and are implemented by a non-governmental private company, the LEED certification is often the measuring standard used by governmental entities most often use to determine whether a building qualifies for green building incentives. LEED uses a 100-point system in which points are awarded based on the design, construction, and maintenance of the construction. The more points awarded to the project, the higher its certification from Certified (40–49 points); to Silver (50–59 points); then to Gold (60–79); and finally Platinum (80–100). The LEED ratings system was first introduced in 1998 and has gone through several iterations and is current in its fourth version (LEEDv4).

It is critical that the parties to a construction project have a clear understanding of who is responsible for ensuring green building compliance. The failure to make it clear up front which party is responsible for LEED compliance can have significant implications if tax incentives are dependent upon certification. Design professionals should be particularly concerned that the owner is not under the impression that the design professional is responsible for compliance when that is not within the scope of work. All of this should be dealt with through clear contractual provisions. For example, the AIA contract between the owner and architect provides that during the design phase the architect will discuss "the feasibility of incorporating environmentally responsible design approaches"[10]; and "shall consider environmentally responsible design alternatives, such as material choices and building orientation."[11] However, obtaining green certification is considered an additional service—and is beyond the scope of basic services in the standard contracts.

E.   OWNERSHIP OF DESIGN DOCUMENTS

Design documents have always been subject to copyright protection under the copyright laws in the United States as a "pictorial, graphic, and sculptural" work which is then defined as "technical drawings, including architectural plans".[12] However,

---

[10]   AIA Doc. B101–2007 § 3.2.3.

[11]   AIA Doc. B101–2007 § 3.2.5.1.

[12]   17 U.S.C. §§ 101 & 102(a)(5).

until 1990 amendments to the Copyright Act, it was unclear whether the unique design aspects of buildings retained their copyright protection after they were built. To demonstrate this dichotomy, in *Jones v. Nino Homes*, the court recognized a valid cause of action by an architect against a builder who made photocopies of a design, but would not find an infringement merely because a builder constructed an identical custom home not based on photocopied blueprints.[13] In 1990, Congress amended the Copyright Act, to extend copyright protection to "architectural work" which is defined as "the design of a building as embodied in any tangible medium of expression, including a building, architectural plans, or drawings. The work includes the overall form as well as the arrangement and composition of spaces and elements in the design, but does not include individual standard features."[14]

The starting point, as a matter of copyright law, then, is that the design professional is the copyright owner of both the design documents as well as the unique design features of the constructed building as well. This, however, can be modified by contract. An issue that arises between an owner and a design professional is who owns design documents. The owner may feel that she hired the design professional to provide a design and therefore the design documents belong to her. The design professional believes that she was retained to

---

[13]   Robert R. Jones Associates, Inc. v. Nino Homes, 858 F.2d 274 (6th Cir. 1988).

[14]   17 U.S.C. § 101.

perform a design service and the resulting plans and specifications remain property of the designer. Most standard agreements say that the design professional retains ownership of the design documents—and the owner has a limited license to use the documents.[15] The license is revocable, which means that the architect can terminate the Owner's use of the license if, for example, the owner fails to pay the architect. ConsensusDocs, however, recognize the possibility of the owner's rights in the design documents themselves and requires an election as to whether the copyright will remain with the design professional or will be transferred to the owner.[16]

If the Owner utilizes design documents on another project despite retention of copyright and the limited license granted to the owner, the architect is particularly concerned that she could be found liable for defects that arise on the new project which she was not hired to evaluate. In those situations, the form contracts take the very practical approach of saying that the owner will indemnify and hold harmless the design professional if the

---

[15]   AIA Doc. B101–2007 § 7.3; EJCDC Doc. § 6.02B & E ("All Documents are instruments of service in respect to this Project, and Engineer shall retain an ownership in property interest therein (including the copyright and the right to reuse at the discretion of the Engineer) whether or not the Project is completed.").

[16]   ConsensusDOCS § 10.1.

designer is sued by a third-party as a result of the unauthorized use of the design documents.[17]

F.   COMMON CONTRACTUAL PROVISIONS IN THE CONTRACT ADMINISTRATION PHASE

The design professional often assists the owner throughout the construction process by providing administrative services. The contract establishes the scope of these services between the owner and design professional—which can be extensive or minimal. The AIA standardized agreement gives an idea of the type and scope of design professional involvement. The architect is involved in evaluation of the work, certification of payment requests from the contractor, reviewing and responding to contractor inquiries regarding the design documents, approving minor changes in the work, and certifying substantial and final completion of the project.

In the administration of the construction phase, the architect's agency is limited to what is expressly set out in the contract. The AIA contract between the owner and contractor provides that the during construction administration the architect acts as the owner's representative, but then says "Architect will have the authority to act on behalf of the Owner only to the extent provided in the Contract Documents."[18] Disputes arise in situations where a

---

[17]   AIA Doc. B101–2007 § 7.3.1; ConsensusDOCS 10.1.3; and EJCDC Doc. § 6.03E.

[18]   AIA A201–2007 § 4.2.1.

contractor seeks additional time or more money from the owner based on representations made by the architect in the course of the project. The owner, citing to the contractual language between the owner and architect (and often reiterated in the contract between the owner and contractor), will point out that the architect did not have the express authority to authorize such a change. In these situations, where the contract does not allow the design professional to authorize the change, the contractor has the burden of demonstrating the architect or engineer, who was not acting within the scope of their **express authority**, was acting with **apparent authority**. This requires actions by the owner that makes it reasonable for the contractor to believe that the design professional had the owner's permission to act. If such apparent authority is found, then the owner is bound by the design professional's actions, but if no such authority is found then the contractor is not entitled to additional compensation. The owner can also be responsible for the work performed by the contractor and authorized by the design professional in contravention of the contract if the owner ratifies the conduct.

A primary benefit to the owner of having the design professional involved in the construction phase of the project is to provide an expert on the ground, responding to questions about ambiguities or inconsistencies in the design documents. The design professional is in the best position to provide guidance or clarification as construction is ongoing.

Another common role that the design professional plays in the course of construction is as the interpreter and arbiter of disputes that arise between the owner and contractor regarding the contract documents.[19] On one hand, this delegation of authority to the design professional is logical—after all, the design professional is intimately familiar with the design documents and how construction is proceeding. On the other hand, expecting the design professional—who is the agent of the owner in other contexts and who is paid by the owner—to resolve disputes between the owner and contractor raises concerns that the design professional has a conflict of interest and cannot be a neutral arbiter of disputes. In response to these concerns, the AIA documents moved from designating the architect as the arbiter to allowing the parties to designate a third party "initial decision maker", with the architect acting if an initial decision maker is not identified.[20] The ConsensusDOCS do not even have the design professional as the default—instead having the parties select either a project neutral or a dispute review board to make findings as to how disputes should be resolved.[21]

---

[19]   EJCDC E–500, Exhibit A, § A1.05(A)(14)(2008).

[20]   AIA A201–2007 § 15.2.

[21]   ConsensusDOCS 200 § 12.3.1 (2011).

G.   LIABILITY OF DESIGN PROFESSIONALS TO THE OWNER (COMMON LAW AND CONTRACT)

A design professional is exactly that—a professional—and is subject to liability under standards of negligence in tort law if they fail to meet the minimum standard of competence in the profession. Therefore, the general common law duty that the architect or engineer owes to the owner is to use that skill and care that a licensed design professional would take under the circumstances. A design that is in violation of a building or housing code is almost always a breach of the design professional's duty, and courts have been willing to find that such violations are **negligence per se**. To establish a breach of the duty the owner ordinarily must come forward with an expert to testify as to how a minimally competent professional, faced with the same circumstances, would have acted differently. These claims arise most often when construction was more expensive or took longer to finish as a result of defective design documents.

In addition to the tort standard of care, it is common for standard contracts to include a contractual standard of care as well. For example, AIA B101–2007 provides: "The Architect shall perform its services consistent with the professional skill and care ordinarily provided by architects practicing in the same or similar locality under the same or similar circumstances."[22] There is similar

---

[22]   AIA Doc. B101–2007 § 2.2.

language in the EJCDC and ConsensusDOCS contracts.[23] There is a belt-and-suspenders sense to these contractual provisions. After all, they set out the essentially the same standard as the common law. However, they also provide a sense of certainty to the parties that they have explicitly agreed to the standard of care. For example, the common law contemplates that the design professional will act as a reasonable design professional would under the circumstances—but where is that reasonable design professional to come from—from the local community or from the larger professional community? The common law is ambiguous—the contractual provision is not—explicitly adopting a locality approach. Furthermore, from a liability standpoint, it is much more difficult to get punitive damages for breach of a contractual provision than in a common law negligence claim. In addition, but explicating setting out the standard that the parties are agree to, it is less likely that a court will impose additional implied obligations on the design professional.

A design professional is also liable to the owner for breach of an express provision of the contract. These claims can and often do overlap—negligent conduct can also breach an express term in the contract—but not always and understanding the difference is important and can impact the right to recovery. For example, assume that the design professional prepares plans that are adequate (non-

---

[23]   EJCDC E–500 § 6.01 (2008); ConsensusDOCS 240 § 2.1 (2011).

negligent) as drafted, but end up being inappropriate for the use the owner wants to put them to. The owner may want to sue the architect for breaching an implied contractual obligation that the plans would be "fit" for the owner's purpose. However, most courts would reject such a claim if the owner cannot cite to an express contractual provision obligating the design professional to ensure fitness, holding that the owner must demonstrate that the architect was negligent in the design and the proper claim is in tort. Understanding this distinction between tort and contract is more than academic. The statute of limitations may vary depending on the type of claim asserted, the proof necessary to establish a claim may be different, and the amount of damages recoverable depends on whether the claim sounds in tort or contract.

H.   LIABILITY OF DESIGN PROFESSIONALS TO THIRD-PARTIES

Construction contracts are similar to other contractual agreements in that one of the primary purposes of the agreements is to shift liability among the various parties. You can imagine that, because of the numerous parties and uncertainties involved in the construction process, design professionals are keenly interested in limiting their liability—particularly to contractors and third-parties with whom they have no contractual relationship. The common liability limitation and liability shifting provisions developed over time in response to court opinions imposing liability on design professionals in different scenarios.

Two common scenarios in which a design professional may be sued by someone they do not have a contractual relationship include where a contractor or subcontractor complains that they suffered increased cost or delay in completion of their work because of defective plans; or where a worker or other third-party argues that they were injured and the injury was the result of defective design. A third situation that has arisen recently and is currently unsettled involves suits disabled persons under the American with Disabilities Act.

1.   LIABILITY TO CONTRACTORS AND SUBCONTRACTORS

A design professional faces two primary types of negligence claims from a contractor or subcontractor. First, those claims that allege negligent design. Second, claims that arise during the administration of the construction process. The difficulty in proceeding on both of these claims is the lack of any contractual relationship between the contractor and the design professional. To demonstrate that the design professional had some obligation (duty) to the contractor, the contractor must be able to point to some obligation owed to the contractor in the agreement between the owner and design professional. The contractor must then be able to demonstrate that the design professional breached that duty and that breach caused the contractor damages.

A design professional that assumes administrative responsibilities in a project must undertake those duties in a competent (non-negligent) manner. A contractor/subcontractor who feels he has suffered loss as a result of a design professional's failure to respond timely to submittals and requests for information, payment requests, or the failure to fairly and objectively resolve disputes, may assert a tort claim. Often the contractor will assert a claim of **negligent misrepresentation** arguing that the design professional made a misrepresentation about some important element of the design which the contractor/subcontractor reasonably relied upon and suffered damage. The design professional may also face a traditional negligence claim—that the design professional was negligent in performing the contractual administration duties.

A significant limitation on the ability of a contractor (or any third-party) to recover from the design professional is the **economic loss doctrine**. This doctrine limits liability for tort claims when the underlying harm is economic loss in performance of a construction contract. Under the doctrine, when a party is dissatisfied with performance under a contract, the remedy is in contract and not tort. Thus, a contractor that has only suffered *economic* losses as the result of the design professional's actions cannot sue in contract because there is no privity, and may be barred from pursuing their claim in tort because of the economic loss doctrine.

2.   LIABILITY TO THOSE WORKING ON JOB SITE

Design professionals are particularly sensitive to being held liable for injuries to those whom they have no relationship with but who are working on the job site—perhaps the employees of a contractor or subcontractor. This arises most often when the design professional has assumed construction administrative obligations. To give an example of the concern, consider the much-cited case of *Miller v. DeWitt*, 226 N.E.2d 630 (Ill. 1967). In that case, three employees of the general contractor were injured when a roof they were working to shore up collapsed. The employees brought a negligence action against the architect. The architect had a standard agreement with the owner that had a "supervision of work" provision which provided that the architect would "endeavor to guard the Owner against defects and deficiencies" in the contractor's work but did not guarantee constant supervision of the project nor the authority to direct the means and methods of construction. The contract also authorized the architect to stop work if the work was not consistent with the contract documents. The Illinois Supreme Court held that the contract language was sufficient to create a duty on the architect to observe the shoring operation and stop work if it was being done unsafely.

It is important to note in cases by employees the claim against the architect is based in tort, but the duty of the architect is found in the language of the contract between the design professional and the owner. In other words, as a general rule, the design professional has no duties to third parties at all. However, if the contract includes that obligation, failure to exercise it in a non-negligent manner can constitute a breach in tort law. The *Miller* case among others, prompted design professionals to reconsider the language used in standard contracts. To this end, the current language setting out architect obligations in the course of construction tends to be indefinite and include a number of disclaimers. For example, the current AIA language is: "The Architect shall not have control over, charge of, or responsibility for the construction means, methods, techniques, sequences or procedures, or for safety precautions and programs in connection with the Work, nor shall the Architect be responsible for the Contractor's failure to perform the Work in accordance with the requirements of the Contract Documents."[24] This is the first line of defense, but a design professional who in fact directs the contractor despite the contractual prohibition may find herself estopped from raising the language as a defense.

3. LIABILITY UNDER THE AMERICANS WITH DISABILITIES ACT

There is a lingering question as to whether a design professional is liable to a disabled individual if the design violates the **Americans With**

---

[24]   AIA Doc. B101–2007 § 3.6.1.2. *See also* EJCDC E–500, Exhibit A, Part A1.05(A)(7)(b); ConsensusDOCS 240 § 3.2.8.4 & 3.2.8.6 (2011).

Disabilities Act (ADA) 42 U.S.C. § 12101 *et seq.* The uncertainty results from the fact that the statute is ambiguous as to exactly who can engage in unlawful "discriminat[ion]" as defined by the statute. One the one hand, Section 302 of the ADA provides that someone who "owns, leases (or leases to), or operates a place of public accommodation" cannot discriminate against the disabled. This section seems to exclude architects—who neither own, lease, nor operate the ultimate building—from coverage under Act. On the other hand, in Section 304, which specifically discusses new construction and alterations in new construction and commercial facilities, discrimination is defined as "a failure to design and construct" a compliant buildings. Courts have split on whether the ADA covers design professionals, with some holding that violations are limited to the Section 302 owners/lessors/operators or that, since architects do not both design *and* construct buildings, they fall outside statutory coverage.[25] Courts holding architects liable have cited to the congressional record and congressional intent that the ADA have broad coverage and rejecting the reading of the statute to require both design and construction as an overly narrow interpretation.[26]

---

[25]   Lonberg v. Sanborn Theaters Inc., 259 F.3d 1029 (9th Cir. 2001); Paralyzed Veterans of America v. Ellerbe Becket Architects & Engineers, P.C., 945 F.Supp. 1 (D.D.C. 1996).

[26]   United States v. Days Inn of America, 997 F.Supp. 1080 (C.D. Ill. 1998).

I.   DESIGN PROFESSIONAL CONTRACTUAL LIMITATIONS OF LIABILITY

It is common for design professionals to limit liability in their contract with the owner. One such provision is a **waiver of consequential damages**. Consequential (as opposed to direct) damages are those that are foreseeable and traceable to the breach but are separate from the contractual breach itself. So, for example, if because of a defective design the owner is delayed in opening the store, the lost profits would be classified as consequential damages. Consequential damages are largely fact dependent and can add a sense of uncertainty as to the extent of potential liability in the event of a breach. The AIA, EJCDC, and ConsensusDOCS contracts include a reciprocal waiver consequential damages provision—meaning that both the owner and the design professional agree to waive consequential damages.[27] Such a provision most often benefits the architect because the owner's consequential damages for a defective design could be significant, while the consequential damages suffered by the design professional if the owner breaches the contract is not likely to be greater than the fee paid under the design agreement.

J.   SUSPENSION OF WORK AND TERMINATION OF CONTRACT

All parties hope that a project will terminate after all services have been rendered and all payment

---

[27]   AIA B101–2007 § 8.1.3; EJCDC E–500 § 6.10(E) (2008); ConsensusDOCS § 5.4.

received. However, relationships do not always end well, and the owner and architect should seek to anticipate and address situations where the contract may be suspended or terminated in their contract to avoid cost and uncertainty. Standard agreements provide explicit guidance on termination.[28] To give an example, the AIA B101–2007 contract provides that if the owner fails to pay the architect the architect can choose to either stop providing services until payment is brought up to date or can terminate the contract.[29] Long-term suspension of the project by the owner (longer than 90 days) is a justification for termination.[30] Either party can terminate the agreement with at least 7 days' notice if the other party fails to perform (and the terminating party is not in breach).[31] The owner is also authorized to terminate the agreement with at least 7 days' notice at the owner's convenience—meaning even if the architect is not in breach. However, if the owner terminates the agreement for convenience, the owner agrees to pay the architect profit and stated expenses.[32] Parties should take into account both what will justify a termination as well as what damages will be due if the contract is terminated.

---

[28]   AIA B101–2007 Art. 9; EJCDC E–500 § 6.05(E) (2008); ConsensusDOCS Art. 8.

[29]   AIA B101–2007 § 9.1.

[30]   AIA B101–2007 § 9.3.

[31]   AIA B101–2007 § 9.4.

[32]   AIA B101–2007 § 9.5–9.7.

CHAPTER 5

THE ROLE OF THE SUBCONTRACTOR

A. INTRODUCTION

Subcontractors play an important role in a construction project, performing most or all of the work on projects of all sizes. The subcontractor has a contractual relationship with the contractor to perform a particular scope of work. This contractual structure means that the owner is one step removed from the subcontractor—the party performing the work on the project. It should come as no surprise that an owner will take steps to ensure that subcontractors perform work in a nondefective manner consistent with the owner's design objectives.

Just as there are standard contracts between the owner/contractor and owner/design professional, there are also standard contracts between the contractor and subcontractor. The same organizations that drafted form contracts in other contexts have also proposed contractor/subcontractor documents, this includes the American Institute of Architects (AIA) contract A401–2007, ConsensusDOCS contract 759, and EJCDC contract C–253. These contracts have the benefit of being well-crafted and well-tested, reducing the likelihood of ambiguity that could arise with custom drafted contracts. The particular disadvantages from the subcontractor's point of view is the fact that the contracts may be drafted to benefit the drafters and are often presented to the subcontractor on a take-it-or-leave-it basis, the length of the contracts may dissuade subcontractors from considering the consequences of all the terms, and, similarly, the contracts may include provisions that are unnecessarily onerous for the subcontractor's limited scope of work on a particular job.

B.   DISTINGUISHING A SUBCONTRACTOR AND SUPPLIER

Categorizing a particular party on a construction job as either a subcontractor or supplier can have a significant impact on the obligations of the party. Stated simply, contracting to provide goods implicates the party is a **supplier** and contracting to supply services indicates that the party is a **subcontractor**. If the party is a supplier, the obligations and warranties under Article 2 of the Uniform Commercial Code (UCC) govern the transaction. On the other hand, if the transaction is for services, traditional common law doctrines apply. Ordinarily, however, categorizing a particular contract as purely goods or purely services is impossible. In these situations, courts look to the nature of the transaction to determine whether it is for services or goods.

Courts have adopted two tests to use when faced with these mixed contracts. The first is the **predominant purpose test**. Under this test, a court will examine the facts of the transaction to determine whether the predominant goal of the contract were the goods (with the services incidental) or services (with goods incidental). To give two classic examples of the distinction, a contract with an artist to paint a room would be a service contract, and a contract to have a hot water heater installed in a bathroom is a sale of goods.[1] The second test, followed by a minority of courts is the **gravamen test**. Under this test, a court will look to the nature of the complaint to identify the nature of the contract. So, for example, where a homeowner hired a contractor to install a propane heater, and the heater ultimately caused a fire, the court will look to the complaint to see if the focus of the allegations are on some defective aspect of the product (fittings or connectors) which would mean the gravamen was the good provided or whether the allegations focus on the workmanship of the contractor in which case the focus would be on services.[2] The importance of this classification is that certain implied warranties and damages are available under the UCC that are not available in a traditional services breach of contract claim. For example, the UCC implies a warranty of merchantability on all sellers of goods and a warranty of fitness for a particular purpose in certain situations.

---

[1]   Van Sistine v. Tollard, 291 N.W.2d 636, 639 (Wis. 1980).

[2]   Anthony Pools v. Sheehan, 455 A.2d 434, 440 (Ct. App. Md. 1983).

C. LICENSING REQUIREMENTS

Subcontractors must be familiar with licensing laws and be aware of when state law requires a subcontractor to have a license to perform work. Failure to have a valid license can have significant consequences. The unlicensed subcontractor may not be able to recover for work performed— regardless of its quality. For example, a Florida statute provides: "As a matter of public policy, contracts entered into . . . , by an unlicensed contractor shall be unenforceable in law or in equity by the unlicensed contractor."[3] The justification for such limitations is to discourage contractors/subcontractors from performing work without a valid license and to ensure that those without licenses do not obtain an unfair advantage over those who go through the expense and time of obtaining a license. Some states, while not allowing enforcement of the contract itself, may be willing to award *quantum merit*. For example, Mississippi's statute provides that performance of work without a valid license renders the contract "null and void." Despite the statutory language, the Mississippi Supreme Court held that an unlicensed subcontractor could recover in *quantum meruit* even though they could not enforce the contract in law.[4] Failure to perform work with a license may also be a criminal offense.

---

[3]   Fla. Stat. § 489.128.

[4]   Ground Control, LLC v. Capsco Industries, Inc., 120 So.3d 365 (Miss. 2013).

D.   SUBCONTRACTOR BIDDING ISSUE

1.   FORMATION OF CONTRACT

Subcontractors are in a precarious position in the bidding process. When a contractor is seeking to submit a bid on a project, she will seek to obtain quotes from various subcontractors and presumably choose the least expensive quote. Unlike the awarding of a prime contract to contractor, there is no set time to consider subcontractor quotes. For this reason, subcontractors often wait until the very last minute to submit a quote to maintain their competitive advantage over other subcontractors. A subcontractor who submits a quote included in the contractor's bid may feel that if the contractor is awarded the contract then the contractor is bound to enter into a contract with the subcontractor. This is not the case. The law considers the quote from the subcontractor to be an offer, and acceptance by the contractor only occurs when the parties enter into a subcontract. Therefore, as a matter of contract law, the contractor is not bound to use the subcontractor whose quote was included in a bid.

It might be logical to think that because the contractor is not bound to use the subcontractor, that the subcontractor whose bid is used would not be bound to honor its quote.[5] While this is the traditional rule, the more modern approach will

---

[5]   See James Baird Co. v. Gimbel Bros., 64 F.2d 344, 346 (2nd Cir. 1933) (Judge Learned Hand)(holding that a subcontractor was not bound to quote because offer was withdrawn before acceptance).

hold the subcontractor to its bid. Relying on the doctrine of **promissory estoppel** courts have adopted what is known as the **firm bid rule** and held subcontractors to the quotes submitted to the contractor and included in the contractor's bid. One of the earliest and often-cited cases to recognize promissory estoppel in this context is the California case *Drennan v. Star Paving Co.*[6] In that case a contractor submitted a bid to build a school. Star Paving submitted a quote for the paving portion of the project. After being awarded the job, Drennan sought to enter into a contract with Star Paving who refused. Drennan then contracted with another paving company at a higher price and sought to recover the difference between Star Paving's quote and the amount Drennan ultimately paid. The court recognized that there was no contract formed because Star Paving attempted to withdraw the quote/offer prior to acceptance by Drennan. However, the court citing to Restatement (Second) of Contracts § 90, held that Star Paving made a promise (its quote) which it could expect to induce action by Drennan (inclusion of the quote in its bid), and which Drennan did reasonably rely on (Drennan had no reason to believe that Star Paving would not honor their bid), therefore, as a matter of equity, Star Paving was estopped from withdrawing their offer for a reasonable time. The court held Star Paving liable for the difference between its bid and the amount Drennan ultimately had to pay for the paving work.

---

[6]   333 P.2d 757 (Cal. 1958).

A critical element of promissory estoppel is that the contractor's reliance must be reasonable. Therefore, if the contractor has reason to know that the subcontractor's quote was incorrect—perhaps because it is so much less than other quotes—it would not be reasonable for the contractor to rely on it, and promissory estoppel would not apply. Or if the subcontractor's quote expressly provides that it is revocable then contractor reliance is not reasonable.

Another element required under § 90 is that justice requires enforcement. Courts have held that where the contractor acted in bad faith (for example waiting an unreasonably long time before accepting offer) promissory estoppel would not apply. Other situations where a court may find that promissory estoppel is not applicable, is when the contractor attempts to leverage the quote to get a lower quote. This can be accomplished in several ways. Where a contractor seeks to find another subcontractor willing to do the work for less than the original subcontractor a practice known as **bid shopping**. The advantage for the contractor is that it has the price ceiling of the bound subcontractor and can retain the profits if it can find a subcontractor to do the work for less. **Bid chiseling** is where the contractor attempts to negotiate down the subcontractor after being awarded the contract. **Bid peddling** is when subcontractors whose quote was not included in the bid originally lobby the contractor seeking to undercut the original subcontractor.

2. SUBCONTRACTOR LISTING STATUTES

One way to limit the perceived inequities of bid shopping and bid peddling is to require the contractor to list the subcontractors she intends to use in the bid itself and require approval of the owner to the substitute. Some states have adopted statutes that require the listing of subcontractors on public projects. These are known as **subcontractor listing statutes**. With regard to private projects, the issue is left to the discretion of the owner.

E. COMMON SUBCONTRACTOR OBLIGATION: FLOW DOWN CLAUSE

One provision in a subcontract can cause endless disputes. Known as **"Flow Down"** provisions, it provides that the subcontractor agrees that its contractual obligations will include those that "flow down" from the owner to the contractor. For example, the AIA form subcontract agreement (A401–2007) Art. 2, entitled "Mutual Rights and Responsibilities" provides that subcontractor "shall assume toward the Contractor all obligations and responsibilities that which the Contractor, under [the Contract Documents], assumes toward the Owner and the Architect." Provision such as this make it critical that subcontractors have copies of all contract documents—including those between the owner and contractor so they can be aware of the obligations that may be imposed on them. For example, in *Keybank National Association v. Southwest Greens of Ohio*, the court held that the subcontractor's lien rights were subordinate to a lender because the terms of the general contract held that the contractor agreed to subordinate its lien rights.[7]

Flow down provision make sense from the standpoint of the owner and contractor because the owner wants to ensure that everyone working on the project follows the owner's design and performance requirements, and the contractor wants to ensure that any obligations it assumes to the owner, the subcontractor is obligated to provide to the contractor. Without these provisions, there could be conflicting obligations between the various parties on the project. To give an example, in *Werner v. Ashcraft Bloomquist, Inc.*, the owner was looking to remodel a shopping center.[8] Part of the contract with the general contractor provided for removal and reinstallation of the shopping center sign. The contractor entered into a subcontract for the sign removal and reinstallation. The subcontract did not contain a flow down provision. Thereafter, the owner, pursuant to the change order provision contained in the general contract, decided to install new signage instead of reinstalling the old signs. Thereafter, the general contractor terminated the agreement with the subcontractor—paying only for the removal portion of the contract. The subcontractor sued and won its breach of contract claim. The court noted that there was nothing in the subcontract that would justify the general contractor changing the scope of work/terminating

---

[7]   988 N.E.2d 32 (Ohio Ct. App. 2013).

[8]   10 S.W.3d 575 (Mo. App. Ct. 2000).

the contract. If there had been a flow down provision in that case, the contractor could have asserted that the subcontractor was subject to the change in the scope of work through a change order to the same extent as the contractor.

So long as the flow down provisions relate solely to the scope of the subcontractor's work, then the overarching concern that everyone is on the same page of the plans and specifications is satisfied. Problems arise, however, when the provision is open-ended and indiscriminate. It purports to flow down *all* or an unspecified amount of the contractor's obligations to the owner to the contractor/subcontractor relationship. This, of course, cannot be the intent of the parties. The question that arises, then, is what terms of the prime contract actually flow down to the subcontractor. Does it include indemnity, claim, dispute resolution provisions? One court held that a no-damage for delay clause included in the general contract was incorporated into the subcontract through the flow down provision.[9] What if there is a conflict between the terms of the contract between the owner and contractor and the contract between the contractor/subcontractor—which provision prevails? To avoid these interpretation issues, contracts should have explicit language concerning what provisions flow down and a clause providing what provision prevails in the event of a conflict. For example, the AIA form subcontract provides,

---

[9]   L&B Construction v. Ragan Enterprises, 482 S.E.2d 279 (Ga. 1997).

where there are inconsistent provisions, the subcontract agreement governs.[10]

F. SUBCONTRACTOR WARRANTIES

1. EXPRESS WARRANTIES

An express warranty is one assumed within the contractual agreement itself. A standard warranty provision states that the subcontractor will perform its scope of work in a good and workmanlike manner free from defects in conformance with the construction documents.[11] There is also typically a provision setting out the length of the warranty after some point—perhaps substantial completion or final completion. The AIA subcontract agreement provides for a one year warranty period from the time of substantial completion.[12] Although this 1 year provision is not in the 2007 version of the AIA form subcontract agreement, it would be implied through the flow-down provision.

When a contract contains a specific warranty time frame, it raises issues regarding the nature of the warranty period. Is it in essence a private limitations period that bars defective claims after the warranty expires (even if it is well short of the applicable statute of limitations) or is it merely an additional contractual obligation which overlaps the general statute of limitations in tort and/or contract. Most courts hold that the contractual provision does

---

[10]   AIA A401–2007, Art. 2.

[11]   AIA A401–2007 § 4.5; A201–2007 § 3.5.

[12]   AIA A201–2007 § 12.2.2.

not work to limit the general statute of limitations. That means that even after the warranty period has passed the owner/contractor can bring a claim for defective work so long as it is not barred by the general statute of limitations.

2.   IMPLIED WARRANTIES

One of the primary reasons it is important to distinguish whether a subcontract is for services or goods is because the Uniform Commercial Code applies to the sale of goods and imposes certain implied warranty obligations as a matter of law. The UCC implies warranties such as the a warranty of merchantability, and the warranty of fitness for a particular purpose, among others.[13]

For service contracts (those not predominantly for the sale of goods), the implied obligations are not generally codified like those in the UCC, but are stated in general terms requiring "workmanlike" construction. For residential dwellings a jurisdiction may also imply into the contract a warranty of habitability. Jurisdictions are split over whether those with no contract with the subcontractor (including the owner and subsequent owners) may sue a subcontractor for breach of these implied warranties. Some courts have found that the policy justifications that exist for extending liability to remote purchasers against the contractor exists with regard to subcontractors, but most states have

---

[13]   UCC § 2–314 (merchantability); § 2–315 (fitness for a particular purpose).

found that lack of privity is a bar to bringing suit.[14] Illinois has the unique rule that recovery is barred unless the contractor is shown to be insolvent.[15] In jurisdictions where lack of privity bars breach of warranty claims against the subcontractor, the aggrieved party's remedy is to sue the contractor who can then seek indemnity from the subcontractor. Attempts to disclaim these warranties, while possible, are difficult to enforce in practice, and courts will look for ways to avoid enforcement.[16]

When the cause of action for breach of an implied warranty accrues—that is when the **statute of limitations** begins to run—depends on the nature of the warranty. For the sale of goods, the UCC provides that the statutory four year statute of limitations begins to run when the tender of delivery of the goods is made.[17] For the common law implied warranties the time is generally governed by the **discovery rule** which provides that the statute begins to run when the defect was or should have been discovered. In some jurisdictions the statute begins to run upon occupancy or substantial completion. Because defects can exhibit many years after completion, a number of jurisdictions have also

---

[14]   Abner Corp. v. City Roofing, 326 S.E.2d 632 (N.C. App. Ct. 1985) (claim allowed); Yanni v. Tucker Plumbing, Inc., 312 P.3d 1130 (Ariz. Ct. App. 2013) (claim barred).

[15]   Minton v. Richards Group of Chicago, 452 N.E.2d 835 (Ill. Ct. App. 1983).

[16]   Bruner & O'Connor Construction Law § 9:74.

[17]   UCC § 2–725. Under the UCC the parties can agree to shorten the statute to one year, but cannot extend it.

adopted a **statute of repose** that limits the right to bring a cause of action. The statutes of repose provide that after a certain number of years all claims for defective construction are barred even if the claim has not yet accrued. For example, Mississippi has a six year statute of repose that begins running "after the written acceptance or actual occupancy or use" of the structure.[18] Under this statute, if an owner discovered a latent defect seven years after initial occupancy, the claim is barred not by the statute of limitations (which started to run upon discovery) but by the statute of repose. There are very few exceptions to the repose period, but one exception is when the contractor is guilty of fraudulent concealment of the defect.

G. SUBCONTRACTOR CLAIM PROCESS AND PASS THROUGH CLAIMS

If a subcontractor believes she is entitled to additional compensation or additional time for work performed on a project, she can make a "claim" to the contractor. To the extent these claims are made against the contractor because of the actions of the contractor, they are resolved between those two parties. However, when the subcontractor makes a claim based on the actions of a third-party (i.e. the owner), the situation becomes more difficult. The AIA contract provides that if the claim by the subcontractor is one that the contractor will have to submit to the owner then the subcontractor must provide notice to the contractor at least two working

---

[18]   Miss. Code Ann. § 15–1–41 (West 2014).

days preceding the date that the contractor's claim is due to the owner.[19]

A subcontractor that has suffered loss at the hands of the owner ordinarily cannot bring a claim against the owner/design professional because there is no contractual relationship between them and the economic loss doctrine would bar the claim. So, the subcontractor is left with the option of pursuing a claim against the contractor—who then can seek indemnity from the owner. Proceeding in this manner is not ideal for the subcontractor. In such a case, the contractor has an incentive to push blame off on the subcontractor in order to avoid having to pay—putting the contractor and subcontractor at odds even when they may ultimately agree that the fault lies with the owner. One way for the contractor and sub-contractor to handle these situations is **pass-through claims**.

This approach is what it sounds like—the contractor will assert (pass through) the claims of the subcontractor against the owner. Because the contractor has a contractual relationship with the owner, this eliminates the economic loss doctrine problem. Of course, such a pass-through relationship is inappropriate if the contractor believes the fault for the delay or damages lies with the subcontractor. However, using this approach eliminates the contentious relationship that arises when the subcontractor is required to go against the contractor. Both the contractor and subcontractor

---

[19]   AIA A401–2007 § 5.3.

can agree that each performed in accordance with
the contract documents and the fault lies solely with
the owner. This is often done through a **liquidating
(or liquidation) agreement.** In the agreement the
contractor agrees to convey to the subcontractor any
money that the contractor receives for the damages
suffered by the subcontractor. The subcontractor
agrees not to pursue the contractor for any
additional amounts. Of course the contractor
assumes a duty to act in good faith in pursuing the
subcontractors claims under the agreement and can
be held liable to the subcontractor for breaching
that duty.

There is a significant limitation on the right to
assert a pass-through claim. This limitation was
first recognized by the U.S. Court of Claims in
Severin v. U.S., 99 Ct. Cl. 435 (1943), and has been
adopted by a majority of states. The basic premise of
the *Severin* **doctrine** is that a pass-through claim
is not available when the subcontractor has no right
to recover from the contractor—and therefore there
is no claim to pass through. For example, *Severin*
involved construction of a post office. Severin, the
general contractor, entered into a subcontract for
exterior work on the post office. The subcontract
contained the following language: "The Contractor
. . . shall not in any event be held responsible for
any loss, damage, detention, or delay caused by the
Owner. . . ." It was undisputed that the project was
delayed due to the actions of the owner. The
contractor brought suit against the owner and
sought to pass through the subcontractor's claim.
The court denied recovery for the pass-through

claim because of the language in the contract there was no valid claim to pass-through. Thus, the Severin doctrine holds that if the subcontractor has agreed that the contractor will not be liable for the damages it has suffered—whether because of contractual agreement or because of settlement— the contractor will not be able to assert a pass-through claim.

H. SCOPE OF WORK, EXTRA WORK AND CHANGES

The "scope of work" is what the subcontractor is agreeing to do for the contract sum. Subcontractors face a unique challenge with regard to defining the scope of work. This is because the subcontractor initially provides a bid to the contractor for the contractor to use in its bid based upon the bid documents. Once the bid is accepted, the subcontractor enters into a contract with the contractor—and that contract will contain a scope of work provision. The subcontractor will want to ensure that the scope of work provision is precise and coincides with what the subcontractor bid to perform. While the subcontractor will prefer a scope of work that is narrowly tailored and specific, the contractor will prefer to have more leeway in the scope of work, and will prefer language such as "all work incidental to" the scope of work. Such language benefits the contractor by allowing the contractor to include within the contract certain work that the subcontractor believes is extra or changed work.

When a subcontractor performs work beyond what was agreed to in the original contractual arrangement, the subcontractor is entitled to additional compensation for this extra work. On the other hand, the contractor should have notice of work that a subcontractor is claiming as extra—and the right to challenge the claim for additional compensation if the contractor feels the work actually falls within the original scope of work. Standardized contracts provide procedures for a subcontractor to give notice to a contractor that the subcontractor is claiming additional compensation. These often require written notification to the contractor. Failure to follow these notice requirements provide the contractor a defense to a claim without having to address the underlying merits of the work performed. In the course of a construction project oral changes—with the promise to later put in writing—occur often. While courts have sometimes allowed subcontractors to recover based on doctrines such as waiver or ratification the subcontractor runs the risk of being denied recover if they fail to follow the contractual notice requirements.[20]

---

[20]   Effect of stipulation, in private building or construction contract, that alterations or extras must be ordered in writing, 2 A.L.R. 3d 620.

I. PAYMENT ISSUES

1.   PAYMENT PROCESS

The first payment issue a subcontractor should consider is the process for obtaining payment. A subcontractor's failure to follow the process set out in the contract to obtain payment can provide contractor a justification for delaying payment. Therefore, the subcontractor should be aware of when payment requests are required, the form the request must be in, and to whom the request must be given. The subcontractor should also be aware of any contractual provisions that provide the contractor a right to withhold payment. Typical provisions justifying withholding of payment include the subcontractor's failure to perform the work and performance of defective work.

2.   PROMPT-PAYMENT STATUTES

A primary concern of subcontractors is that the contractor will not pay them in a timely manner. These concerns are great enough that many states have adopted **prompt-payment statutes**. These laws require contractors to pay subcontractors for work performed within a certain number of days after receiving payment from the owner. The statutes provide penalties if the contractor fails to make payment in a timely manner. They also include circumstances where a contractor is justified in delaying payment—such as when the subcontractor has failed to perform or has performed in a defective manner.

3.   CONTINGENT PAYMENT PROVISIONS: PAY-WHEN-PAID AND PAY-IF-PAID PROVISIONS

Some subcontracts include clauses that attempt to make payment to the subcontractor contingent on the contractor receiving payment for the subcontractor's work from the owner. These provisions can be classified as either "**pay-if-paid**" or "**pay-when-paid**." The difference between the "if" and "when" is crucial and depends on how the clause is drafted. A pay-*if*-paid provision contains a clear contingency that the subcontractor will only be paid if the contractor receives payment from the owner. The consequence, of course, is that the subcontractor could receive payment only long after work has been performed and runs the risk of receiving no payment. On the other hand, if interpreted as a pay-*when*-paid clause it means that the contractor can only withhold payment from the subcontractor for a reasonable time waiting on payment from the owner, and after that reasonable amount of time must make payment to the subcontractor even if the contractor has not received payment.

The concern that courts have with pay-if-paid clauses is that it places the burden of non-payment by the owner on the subcontractor—who has no contractual relationship with the owner. Thus, a subcontractor that has fully performed in a good and workmanlike manner may be denied payment by a solvent contractor with whom they have a contract because the owner is withholding payment from the contractor. Due to this inequity some jurisdictions have held that these provisions violate public policy and refuse to enforce them.[21] Even in those jurisdictions where courts have been willing to enforce these provisions, they only do so when the language is explicit and admits to no ambiguity. As one court stated, interpreting a provision to be a pay-when-paid clause, these provisions conditioning payment on receipt from the owner, "are not intended to provide the contractor with an eternal excuse for nonpayment."[22]

If courts can find any ambiguity in the contractual language, they will read it as a pay-when-paid and not a pay-if-paid clause. For example, in *Thomas J. Dyer Co. v. Bishop International Engineering Co.*, the court interpreted the following language to be a pay-when-paid clause: "The total price to be paid to the Subcontractor shall be . . . , no part of which shall be due until five (5) days after Owner shall have paid Contractor. . . ." The court reasoned that the intent of the parties must have been that the subcontractor would be paid within a reasonable amount of time for the work performed because there was no explicit contingency stating that the subcontractor would only be paid if the owner was insolvent and did not pay the contractor for the subcontractor's

---

[21]   West-Fair Electric Contractors v. Aetna Casualty & Ins., 87 N.Y.2d 148 (N.Y. Ct. App. 1995) (invalid under state lien law); William R. Clarke Corp. v. Safeco Ins. Co., 938 P.2d 372 (Cal. 1997) (same).

[22]   Midland Engineering Co. v. John A. Hall Construction Co., 398 F.Supp. 981, 993 (N.D. Ind. 1975).

work. On the other hand, a federal district court faced with this language: "It is specifically understood and agreed that the payment to the subcontractors is dependent, as a condition precedent, upon the contractor receiving payments, including retainer from the Owner", held that the condition was sufficiently explicit to make payment to the subcontractor contingent.[23]

J.   DISPUTE RESOLUTION

Disputes between a contractor and subcontractor can be resolved either through a mechanism set out in the contract or through a court process. Often, the contract will provide a step-by-step process for dispute resolution. For example, the AIA subcontract agreement provides that any disputes must first go to mediation, and if mediation is not successful, then either to arbitration or to litigation. ConsensusDOCS adds the requirement of "good faith discussions" to attempt to resolve any disputes before submitting to mediation and then arbitration or litigation.[24]

The contract may also set out a forum for any disputes and the law to be applied if a dispute arises. ConsensusDOCS states that the location of dispute resolution and the choice of law to be applied is the jurisdiction where the project is located.[25] An out of state contractor, however, may

---

[23]   Architectural Systems, Inc. v. Gilbane Building Co., 760 F.Supp. 79, 80 (D. Md. 1991).

[24]   ConsensusDOCS 750 § 11.3

[25]   ConsensusDOCS 750 §§ 11.5; 12.3.

wish to have the arbitration or litigation occur in the contractor's home state instead of where the contract is located. Whether these venue provisions are enforceable depends on the jurisdiction. Some states have passed laws that such provisions are unenforceable.[26]

Another important issue to consider is the party that will bear attorney's fees. The **American Rule** is that each party bears their own attorney's fees. This general rule can be modified by contract or by statute. Therefore, a contractual provision shifting attorney's fees to the non-prevailing party are enforceable. The AIA form subcontract agreement does not contain an attorney fees provision. On the other hand, ConsensusDOCS provides that the non-prevailing party is responsible for attorney's fees.[27]

K. TERMINATION

The justifications for terminating a subcontract are often set out in the contract itself. If the parties have not agreed contractually to the justifications for termination, the common law requirement of a material breach or a defense to performance must exist. Because of the interrelated nature of the construction contracts and the dependence of the various parties to the project, it behooves all parties to set out the bases and consequences of termination. To demonstrate how the interrelated nature of the parties can justify unique contract

---

[26]   Va. Code § 8.01–262.1.

[27]   ConsensusDOCS 750 § 11.4.

provisions, consider the situation where the contract between the owner and contractor is terminated, but the owner wishes to continue construction with the subcontractors doing work on the project. Of course the owner has no contractual relationship with the subcontractors. To address this issue, standard contracts provide that if the owner terminates the contractor, the owner has the right to an **assignment of the subcontract** agreements—thus stepping into the shoes of the contractor.[28] In turn, the subcontract obligates the subcontractor to accept assignment of the subcontract.[29]

1.   BY THE CONTRACTOR

The first issue with regard to termination of a subcontractor by the contractor is whether there are any contractual or policy limitations on the termination. For example, the jurisdiction's subcontractor listing statute may limit the right of termination. Contractually, if the owner directed the contractor to use a particular subcontractor, the contractor may not be able to terminate/substitute the subcontractor over the owner's objection.[30]

a. Termination for Cause

Termination for cause (or fault) is termination for failure of the subcontractor to perform under the subcontract. The AIA form subcontract provides

---

[28]   AIA A201 § 5.4.1; ConsensusDOCS 200 § 5.4.1.

[29]   AIA A401 § 7.4.1; Consensus DOCS 750 § 10.5.

[30]   AIA A201–2007 § 5.2.4

that the contractor must give the subcontractor 10 days' notice and an opportunity to cure before terminating.[31] Some courts have held that even if there is not a specific contractual provision allowing a time to cure, it will be implied as an obligation of the duty of good faith and fair dealing.[32] The contractor who terminates the subcontractor for cause can complete the work and charge the subcontractor the difference between the amounts owed to the subcontractor and the cost to finish the job.[33] It is easy to see where disputes will arise over whether the subcontractor actually failed to perform, and the contractor does run the risk in a dispute that the fact-finder will rule in favor of the subcontractor and find that the contractor did not have a valid basis for terminating for cause. If that is the case, the contractor will be in material breach and the subcontractor can seek damages—even those damages excluded by the contract itself. To avoid this, ConsensusDOCS includes a provision which states that in the event the contractor inappropriately terminates the subcontract for cause, the contractor is only liable for those damages a subcontractor would be entitled to if the contract had been terminated for convenience.[34]

---

[31]   AIA A401–2007 § 7.2.1; ConsensusDOCS 750 § 10.1.1.

[32]   McClain v. Kimbrough Const. Co., Inc., 806 S.W.2d 194 (Ct. App. Tenn. 1990).

[33]   AIA A401–2007 § 7.2.1.

[34]   ConsensusDOCS § 10.7.

b. Termination for Convenience

Termination of a contract for convenience is when the contract is terminated other than for cause. Without a provision allowing for such termination, the termination would constitute a breach of contract by the terminating party. The AIA documents contemplate that the contractor can terminate the subcontract for convenience in two situations. The first is when the owner terminates the general contract for convenience. In these situations, the contractor has the right to terminate the subcontract. The subcontractor must cease operations, take steps to preserve the work performed, terminate all future sub-subcontracts and material or supply contracts.[35] The subcontractor is entitled (under the AIA documents) to: payment for work performed, cost incurred as a result of the termination, and reasonable overhead/profit for the remaining work under the contract.[36] On the other hand, the ConsensusDOCS limit the subcontractor's right to recover to what the contractor can actually recover from the owner on the subcontractor's behalf.[37]

The subcontract could also provide that the contractor could terminate the subcontract for convenience. If that were the case, the subcontractor would be entitled to recover the damages designated in the contract. However, the standardized contracts

---

[35]   AIA A401–2007 § 7.2.2–7.2.3.

[36]   AIA A401–2007 § 7.2.4.

[37]   ConsensusDOCS 750 § 10.4.

do not provide contractor convenience as a justification for terminating a subcontract. Instead, they contemplate that the contractor only has the right to suspend work for convenience (and the subcontractor is entitled to an adjustment of time or money based on the suspension).[38]

2.   BY THE SUBCONTRACTOR

The subcontractor also has the right to terminate the contract. If there are no contractual provisions setting out the basis for termination, the subcontractor must demonstrate material breach by the contractor or a valid defense to performance. The form contracts set out specific bases for the subcontractor to terminate the contract. The AIA document provides that the subcontractor can terminate the subcontract for the same reasons that the contractor can terminate its contract with the owner. In addition, the provision expressly provides that the subcontractor can terminate the subcontract if the contractor has not made payments within 60 days of amounts becoming due.[39] ConsensusDOCS takes a more subcontractor-friendly approach. If the subcontractor's work has been stopped because the subcontractor "has not received progress payments or has been abandoned or suspended for an unreasonable period of time" the subcontractor may terminate the subcontract with seven days written notice.[40]

---

[38]   AIA A401–2007 § 7.3; ConsensusDOCS 750 § 10.6.

[39]   AIA A401–2007 § 7.1.

[40]   ConsensusDOCS 750 § 10.8.

The AIA subcontract agreement provides that if the subcontractor validly terminates the subcontract, the subcontractor is entitled to payment for work performed, costs incurred because of the termination (limited to demobilization costs), including overhead and damages for the work performed.[41] The ConsensusDOCS on the other hand allow the subcontractor more damages (including attorney's fees) when non-payment is the fault of the contractor, and less damages when the failure to pay is the result of someone other than the contractor.[42] As in all situations where a party is alleging breach of contract which excuses performance, the decision to declare a contract terminated for cause is risky. There is always the possibility that the fact-finder will determine that there was not sufficient evidence of a breach to justify termination.

L.   LIEN RIGHTS AND STOP PAYMENT NOTICE RIGHTS

Subcontractors face an unenviable position on a construction project. The subcontractor provides goods and services that are incorporated into a project that will be used by the owner, but the subcontractor has no contractual relationship with the owner. This means, as a matter of common law, the subcontractor must rely and look to the contractor for payment or rely on such uncertain common law claims as unjust enrichment. To

---

[41]   AIA A401–2007 § 7.1

[42]   ConsensusDOCS 750 § 10.8

address this, states grant subcontractors **lien rights** as a matter of statute (these are often referred to as **mechanic's liens**). A lien is the assertion of a legal interest in a particular piece of property. In the case of subcontractors it is asserted against property on which work was performed. The lien is filed as a matter of public record to give third-parties notice of the interest. When a valid lien is asserted, the owner cannot sell the property—and likely cannot mortgage it—without satisfying the lien. Ultimately if the lien is not satisfied the claimant can seek to foreclose on the property to satisfy the lien. Thus, in those jurisdictions where lien rights are available they are a powerful tool available to the subcontractor to motivate an owner to ensure that subcontractors are paid by the contractor to avoid liens on the property.

Lien rights are purely a statutory creation at the state level and are strictly construed by courts. Because every state has a different law, those wanting to assert lien rights must pay close attention to ensure that they understand both the procedural and substantive provisions of the law. Procedurally, the laws often require notice to be given before a lien can be filed in the public records. The notice must be filed in the right location (typically where the property is located). It must also be filed within the designated time—often within a certain amount of time after the last work is performed on the project. Finally, the burden is on the claimant to seek to enforce the lien within a certain amount of time or lose the right.

Substantively, only those expressly listed in the lien statute have the right to file a lien. For example, some states only give lien rights to contractors or those with a direct contract with the owner—and not subcontractors. Others only extend lien rights to first-tier subcontractors or suppliers. In addition to limitations on who can file a lien, there are also limitations on the type of property that can be liened. The universal rule is that only private property—not public property—is subject to a lien.

1.   LIEN WAIVER

The owner on a construction contract has certain fundamental objectives—such as having the project completed consistent with the construction documents on time and within budget. Of equal concern is ensuring that everyone performing work on the project is paid for work performed so that the property is burdened with liens. The problem for the owner is that she does not have a contract with those supplying labor or supplies on the project, and must rely on the contractor to distribute payments consistent with the work performed. One way that owners seek to address this problem is by requiring lien waivers with payment to the contractor. Lien waivers contemplate that a subcontractor will not assert a lien for work previously performed. A valid lien waiver will negate the right to assert a lien—thus, protecting the owner's property interest.

To avoid the potential harm caused by a lien filed on the property, an owner may want to have those performing work on the property to prospectively waive lien rights. This would waive the right to assert a lien prior to any work being performed. As a matter of public policy some jurisdictions have declared these types of waivers unenforceable.

2.   OWNER DEFENSES TO A LIEN

The owner can defeat a lien by demonstrating the claimant is not in the class protected by the lien statute, that the claimant failed to follow the procedural requirements to assert a claim, or that there was a valid lien waiver executed for the claimed amount. In addition, there are other defenses that an owner may be able to assert depending on the jurisdiction. If the owner paid the contractor prior to receiving notice of the lien, the owner may have a defense to assertion of a lien (although in some jurisdictions the owner will be held responsible even if the contractor was paid). The wrongful filing of a lien may also result in penalties either under the lien statute itself or damages as a result of a tort action such as **slander of title**.

3.   STOP PAYMENT NOTICE

In some jurisdictions a subcontractor, even if not entitled to assert a lien against the project property, may be entitled to assert a claim against funds in the hands of the owner that have not yet been paid to the contractor. The statutes creating these rights are commonly known as **Stop Notice statutes**. These rights are purely a matter of statute and those entitled to assert stop notice rights and how to assert the rights vary by state. However, a key attribute of these rights is that it puts the owner on notice that the claimant is entitled to payment and has not been paid by the contractor. At that point, the owner must refrain (stop) any further payments to the contractor until receiving assurance that the claimant has been paid. If the owner receives notice and afterward issues a payment to the contractor, the owner becomes liable to the claimant and may be subject to double payment. It is important to note that these statutes only apply to funds that remain in the hands of the owner at the time notice is provided. The claimant cannot claim an interest in the amounts the owner has already paid to the contractor.

Stop notice statutes protect the claimant but it also impacts the contractor by withholding all payments to the contractor. This raises potential due process concerns because, if the claimant only has to assert a claim to freeze the funds, then the contractor is not given an opportunity to demonstrate why the claimant may not be entitled to the amounts alleged. For this precise reason, the Fifth Circuit in *Noatex v. King Construction of Houston*, held Mississippi's stop notice statute unconstitutional—it withheld/deprived the money due to the contractor for an indefinite period of time without an opportunity for a hearing on whether the amounts were properly being withheld.[43] The court found the lack of procedural safeguards as

---

[43]   732 F.3d 479 (5th Cir. 2013).

constitutionally fatal. Other states have more detailed procedural requirements that may survive constitutional scrutiny.[44]

---

[44]   See Cal. Civ. Code §§ 3156 *et seq.*

CHAPTER 6

THE ROLE OF THE SURETY

A. INTRODUCTION

A surety relationship is not unique to the construction industry. In fact there is an entire Restatement on Suretyship and Guaranty. Suretyship simply represents a situation in which one person agrees to perform or to pay a debt owed by another if they fail to perform. This relationship could arise in any area of life. In the construction context, sureties are companies that issue **surety bonds** agreeing if the contractor defaults in performance or payment under the construction documents, the surety will step in and either make payments due to those providing work on the project or to complete the project. The goal of this chapter is to identify the parties in the surety context and examine the rights and responsibilities of the parties.

B. TRIPARTITE RELATIONSHIP

In a surety relationship there are three parties—the **surety**, **principal**, and **obligee**. This is commonly referred to as a **tripartite relationship** and each of the parties have some rights/obligations to the other parties. The surety and the contractor will enter into a contract, known as a surety bond, in which the surety promises the obligee (owner) that the surety will step in if the principal (contractor) fails to perform its obligations under the construction documents. Thus, the involvement of the surety on a construction contract is for the benefit and protection of the owner. The surety is only obligated to expend funds to the extent set out in the bond document. This amount is known as the **penal sum** or **penalty sum** of the bond. There are four primary types of surety bonds issued in the construction context: bid bond, payment bond, performance bond, and lien bond. Federal law, under the **Miller Act**, 40 U.S.C. §§ 3131–3134, requires both performance and payment bonds on federal construction projects. A number of states follow the lead of the federal government, and require payment and performance bonds on construction projects. These state laws are known as **Little Miller Acts**, but the statutes have unique differences from the federal law. With regard to private projects, the decision of whether to require a payment or performance bond is left up to the owner. The AIA General Conditions recognizes that the owner has the right to require payment and/or performance bonds.[1]

There is a tendency to think of a surety relationship in the same terms as insurance, but they are different. In the insurance context, the insurance company is agreeing with the insured to assume the cost of certain risks in the event those risks occur. So, an individual with automobile insurance is purchasing a policy wherein the insurance company agrees to assume the risk and satisfy any claims that fall within the scope of the

---

[1]   AIA A201–2007 § 11.4.1.

policy up to the policy amounts. The insurance company does not then have the right to try to collect the amounts paid from the insured.

The surety relationship is distinct. As an initial matter the surety relationship involves three parties whereas the insurance contract involves two. Substantively, the surety agrees to step into the shoes of its principal (contractor) in the case of default. After satisfying the bond obligations, however, the surety has the right to seek indemnity from the contractor (often personally) for the amounts paid by the surety to complete the work or to make payments. In this way the surety steps into the shoes of its principal and is only obligated to pay those amounts the principal is obligated to pay. For example, if the contractor has a defense to making payment to a subcontractor, the surety can also assert those defenses to reduce or eliminate the obligation to make payment under a payment bond. When the surety receives a bond claim, it has a contractual obligation to act in a timely manner and an implied obligation to act in good faith. Failure to do so can result in a breach of contract claim or a bad faith tort claim.

C. BID BOND

A **bid bond** is a bond that the owner of a project (particularly of a public project) may demand from a party bidding on a project. The bidder obtains the bond from a surety. The purpose of the bond is to protect the owner in the event the contractor is the lowest and best bidder but refuses to enter into a contract with the owner. At that point the owner is faced with the prospect of having to absorb the cost of rebidding the project. There are two types of bid bonds and the amount that the owner recovers depends on the type of bond that issued. The first is a **damage bond**, which provides that the owner can recover the amount of actual damages suffered up to the penal sum. The second is a **forfeiture bond** in which the owner is entitled to the entire amount of the bond as liquidated damages.[2]

D.   PAYMENT BOND

A **payment bond** is issued by a surety company to guarantee payment to those performing labor or work on the project if the principal fails to make payment. The surety is responsible for payment up to the penal sum of the bond. While payment bonds are required on state and federal projects, the question of whether to require a payment bond on a private project is up to the owner. However, in some jurisdictions, if the owner does require a payment bond, the bond substitutes for lien rights for those covered by the bond.[3] The AIA form performance bond and payment bond document (A312) are commonly used on both public and private projects.

There are a couple of issues to be aware of with regard to a payment bond. The first is the scope of claimants entitled to make a demand for payment on the bond. The AIA form bond agreement defines

---

[2]   Bruner & O'Connor on Construction Law § 7:40.

[3]   See Laughlin Environmental, Inc. v. Premier Towers, L.P., 126 S.W.3d 668, 671 (Tex. Ct. App. 2004).

"claimant" as those: (1) having a direct contractual relationship with the contractor or with a subcontractor; and (2) those with lien rights under the applicable statute. Thus, the AIA document extends protection under the bond to first-tier subcontractors and those with lien rights. State statutes vary with regard to how they define claimant on public projects.

In addition satisfying the definition of a "claimant" the person seeking payment under the payment bond must also have performed work that the bond covers. For example, the AIA Payment Bond covers "labor, materials and equipment furnished for use in performance of the Construction Contract."[4] Therefore, if the claim or part of a claim does not fall into these categories, the surety is not obligated to pay. For example, if "labor" is interpreted to mean only physical labor, a claim for administrative overhead would not be a compensable claim.

A claimant seeking payment pursuant to a payment bond must be aware of the notice and timing prerequisites to asserting a claim. There are two relevant time frames. First, the time to file the initial claim for payment. First tier claimants do not have a designated time to give notice before pursuing a payment bond claim—the rationale is that because there is a contract with the contractor, the contractor should be aware those he is in contract with have not been paid. However, the

---

[4]   AIA A312–2010 § 1.

same is not true for those claimants without a direct contract with the contractor, and the bond requires notice be provided to the contractor within a certain amount of time. For example, the AIA form bond requires that a claimant without a direct contractual relationship with the contractor must have provided notice of non-payment to the contractor within ninety days after performing labor or furnished equipment/materials on the project.[5] The second time frame is a limitations period in which the claimant must seek to enforce a claim in court or through dispute resolution. The AIA Payment Bond provides that the claimant has one year from the date the claimant last performed work on the project or one year from the date that the claim was sent to the surety—whichever time is shorter.[6] Some states have statutes that invalidate these time limits if they are shorter than the jurisdiction's limitation period. If not prohibited, these notice and limitation periods can be raised as defenses by the surety to payment. In addition, the surety can raise all defenses to payment that the contractor could have raised.

E.   PERFORMANCE BOND

Performance bonds are guarantees that the surety will complete the project in compliance with the contract documents if the contractor defaults on performance. Upon receiving notice of default, the surety assumes the obligation to complete the

---

[5]   AIA A312–2007 Payment Bond § 5.1.1.

[6]   AIA A312–2007 Payment Bond § 12.

project. Performance bonds are required on public projects at both the federal and state level. In the private context, the owner has the option to require the contractor to provide a performance bond.[7] With regard to performance, the surety steps into the shoes of the contractor and assumes all of the claims against the owner that the contractor would have had.

According to the terms of the performance bond, it is up to the surety as to how to go about getting to completion, and an owner who interferes with the selection risks losing their rights under the bond contract.[8] The surety may find that it is best to contract with the principal (the defaulting contractor) to finish the project. The surety could also put the remaining work out for bid and tender the new contractor to the owner. The surety also has the option of completing the work itself. A final option is to forgo performance all together and pay the owner/obligee the amount necessary to finish the project.[9] The approach to choose depends on the project. If the contractor defaulted merely because he ran out of money then the surety may choose to finance the contractor to finish the job. If the project is near completion the surety may choose just to pay the owner the cost to finish the job.

---

[7]   AIA A201–2007 § 11.4.1

[8]   St. Paul Fire & Marine Ins. Co. v. City of Green River, 93 F.Supp.2d 1170 (D. Wyo. 2000).

[9]   AIA A312 Performance Bond § 5.

CHAPTER 7

COMMON CONTRACTUAL PROVISIONS

A. INTRODUCTION

There are a number of contractual provisions that are common in construction contracts. These clauses are ubiquitous enough to justify a separate chapter. The provisions addressed include: (a) differing site conditions provision; (b) indemnity provision; (c) change in work provisions; (d) liquidated damages provisions; and (e) insurance provisions.

B. DIFFERING SITE CONDITIONS CLAUSE

The subsurface condition at the project site can be an unknown until construction has commenced and the conditions are exposed. The fact that the subsurface condition cannot be established with certainty until after construction has commenced puts both the contractor and the owner in an unenviable position. Therefore, construction contracts often contain a provision setting out an agreed process for addressing conditions discovered on the site that were not anticipated by the parties.

If there is no differing site condition clause in the contract, a contractor would increase its bid to take into account the possibility that unanticipated site conditions will be encountered—because the contractor would bear the risk (cost) of the unforeseen conditions. The only options to a contractor operating without a differing site conditions clause are the common law claims of misrepresentation if the owner misrepresented the condition of the premises or breach of implied warranty of sufficiency of plans and specifications if they contained express representations of the conditions that were incorrect. By including an agreed upon method of addressing differing site conditions, the contractor can rely on the provision for additional compensation and the owner can avoid paying a contingency amount that might not be necessary.

A common differing site conditions clause is found in the AIA A201–2007 § 3.7.4 (the General Conditions). The provision identifies two different types of differing site conditions. First are **Type I differing site conditions**. Type I conditions are defined as those materially different than indicated in the contract. Therefore, to fall within this category there had to be some representations made regarding the conditions the contractor could expect to encounter. To assert a claim of Type I differing site conditions the contractor must demonstrate that the conditions differed *materially* from what was represented in the contract documents, that the condition was not foreseeable based on a reasonable investigation of the site or interpretation of the contract documents; that the contractor gave sufficient notice as required by the contract; and that the contractor suffered delay and/or incurred additional costs as a result of the condition.

The second type of unanticipated site conditions are **Type II differing site conditions**. These are conditions which are different from what would normally be encountered in performing the particular type of work in the area. To establish a claim for a Type II differing site condition the contractor must show that the condition was unusual and would not have been reasonably anticipated based on the contract documents, inspection of the site, or experience in the area.

An owner may argue that the condition was not materially different from the contract documents or that it was not unusual in the area to avoid paying additional compensation to the contractor. The owner may also argue that a reasonable site inspection would have revealed the condition and the contractor should be held to what a reasonable inspection would have revealed. Some owners have also attempted to disclaim the accuracy of any representations made in the contract documents (and therefore the contractor had the obligation to perform tests to determine the true nature of the site). Courts that have enforced these exculpatory provisions have strictly construed them with any ambiguity interpreted against the owner. The owner may also argue that the contractor failed to provide notice within the proscribed time frame (21 days under the AIA documents) and is barred from recovery.

Subcontractors should also be aware of the differing site conditions clause in the contract between the owner and contractor. A subcontractor that anticipates a particular site condition in submitting its bid will not be able to recover additional compensation when the condition is different than anticipated where it was reasonable foreseeable that the condition would be different than anticipated. Thus, if a site inspection would have revealed the condition, the fact that the subcontractor did not perform such an inspection would be a defense to a claim for increased pay or extended time for the condition.

C.   INDEMNITY PROVISIONS

Indemnity provisions are contractual agreements to pay one party for amounts they are required to pay to a third party. In one sense these liability shifting provisions make sense. If an innocent bystander is injured walking by a construction site solely as a result of a subcontractor's negligence, and the contractor is required to compensate the victim, then the contractor should be able to recover those amounts from the negligent subcontractor. Issues arise, however, when the contractor attempts to shift liability to a subcontractor for harm either not caused by the subcontractor or only partially caused by the subcontractor. Indemnity provisions are often categorized by the scope of indemnification required. Identifying the nature of the indemnity provision is important because states have enacted **Anti-indemnity statutes** that declare certain indemnity provisions unenforceable as a matter of public policy.

1. LIMITED (TYPE III) INDEMNITY PROVISIONS

Type III (limited) indemnity provisions provide that the indemnitor will indemnify only for losses caused by the indemnitor's own negligence. These are the narrowest indemnity provisions. So, for example, if a subcontractor is responsible for installing glass doors and a customer is injured when she runs into the door because the subcontractor negligently failed to place warning labels on the door (and through no fault of the contractor), if the contractor is held liable for the actions of this subcontractor, then the contractor can seek indemnity from the subcontractor for the amounts paid. This is the approach adopted by the AIA documents and other form agreements.[1]

2. INTERMEDIATE (TYPE II) INDEMNITY PROVISIONS

Type II (intermediate) indemnity provisions provide that the indemnitor will be responsible to indemnify for all amounts paid if the indemnitor bears any responsibility for the loss. In other words, if the concurrent actions of the contractor and subcontractor contributed to the loss, the contractor can recover the entire amount paid out from the subcontractor—even if the subcontractor is only 1% at fault. Whether these provisions are enforceable depends on the jurisdiction. Some jurisdictions have enacted **Anti-Indemnity** statutes that invalidate

---

[1]   AIA A401–2007 § 4.6.1; ConsensusDOCS 750 § 9.1.1; EJCDC C–523 § 10.04(A).

Type II indemnity provisions. Even in those jurisdictions where not statutorily prohibited, courts will strictly interpret the provisions—limiting their scope to the extent possible.

3. BROAD (TYPE I) INDEMNITY PROVISIONS

Type I (broad) indemnity provisions are the broadest and, from a public policy perspective, the most troubling. They require one party to indemnify another for any described losses—even if the loss was caused wholly by the party being indemnified. Some jurisdictions have passed **Anti-Indemnity** statutes that make such provisions unenforceable. Even in jurisdictions without such statutory prohibitions, courts are skeptical of such provisions and enforce them strictly.

4. LIABILITY COVERED BY INDEMNITY PROVISIONS

In addition to identifying the overall scope of indemnity provisions, parties should be concerned with the scope of liability covered by the provision. If there is a contractual indemnity provision, courts will look to that provision. For example, the AIA indemnity provision (and provisions in other standardized contracts are similar) provides indemnity for losses "arising out of or resulting from performance of the Subcontractor's Work under this Subcontract, provided that any such claim . . . is attributable to bodily injury sickness, disease or death, or to injury to or destruction of tangible property (other than the Work itself)."[2] This last provision "other than the Work itself" limits indemnity claims to those asserted for losses caused by the subcontractor's work—and does not extend to mere defective performance of the work by the subcontractor. The liability covered in the form contracts is anticipated to be in situations where a third-party is injured as a result of a subcontractor's negligence. In addition to the types of claims the subcontractor is assuming an indemnity obligation, the indemnity provision may also set out the amounts that must be indemnified, which could include attorney's fees and other costs in addition to the actual harm caused.

D. CHANGES IN WORK

Work that deviates from the scope of work can be categorized as either "extra" or "changed" work. **Changed work** occurs when there is some modification to the scope of work itself. Perhaps certain items are added or deleted from the work as described or there is a change in the sequence that the work will be performed. **Extra work** on the other hand is work that is not contemplated within the original scope of work. Understanding the difference between a change and extra work is important because, while both may change the amount of compensation due or the amount of time allotted for completion of the project, they are addressed in different ways in standard contracts.

---

[2]   AIA A401–2007 § 4.6.1

Changes are a necessary part of the organized chaos of a construction project. Unexpected circumstances are certain to arise and all parties are better off if there is a set and expedited mechanism for handling these occurrences. The AIA approach to changes provides a good example of how the interests of the interests of the owner/contractor and the subcontractor are protected. First, it may be that all parties agree to a particular change. In these situations the subcontractor agree to a change in the scope of work with the issuance of a formal **change order**. The agreement includes the change in the work and the amount of additional money/time the change will require.

If the parties cannot reach an initial agreement the project does not stop until the dispute is resolved. Instead, the owner and architect have the right to unilaterally issue a **construction change directive** which requires the contractor to perform the work despite a continuing dispute. The contract then provides the subcontractor a mechanism to seek additional compensation for the change (and to resolve disputes about that claim) separate from the work itself.

1.   "CARDINAL" CHANGE

When a requested change is so far beyond what the parties contemplated under the original contract, it is more than a "change" covered by the changes clause of the contract and is instead a breach of the construction contract. These type of changes are termed **cardinal changes**. If a change

is determined to be cardinal, the limitations on
damage recovery imposed by the contract are no
longer enforced and the contractor is excused from
performance. Of course, identifying a change as
cardinal, and declaring the contract terminated is
risky because the question is fact-dependent and a
reviewing body may determine that the change was
not significant enough to justify the termination. In
that case the contractor has breached the contract
by not performing. The nature of change required
for a finding of cardinal change has been described
as "drastic", "fundamentally alter[ing]" the contract,
or imposing obligations "far exceeding any
contemplated by the contract."

2.   CONSTRUCTIVE CHANGE

A **constructive change** is a change that is
neither memorialized in a change order nor
unilaterally directed by the owner. Instead, it is a
change which imposes an obligation on the
contractor to do work outside the scope of the
contract, but which the owner does not recognize as
a change at all. Because there is no formal change
order or change directive issued, the contractor
must look to the claim provision of the contract to
assert the right to additional time or payment
rather than the change provision.[3]

Constructive changes occur when the owner or
the owner's agent take action that result in
additional costs or the need for additional time by

---

[3]   AIA A201–2007 § 15.3.

the contractor. For example, where the plans or specifications are defective and the contractor has to do additional work as a corrective, that is a constructive change because the contractor agreed to perform the scope of work set out in the contract and work necessary because of defective plans/specifications is beyond the scope of work agreed to. The same rationale is true where the owner rejects work that is in accordance with the contract documents. If the contractor is successful in a claim for a constructive change, the contractor is entitled to additional compensation for the work and/or additional time as a result of the delay caused by the change.

Contractors should always follow the contractual procedures for asserting a claim for a change in the scope of work. However, courts have been willing to allow the contractor's claim to go forward despite the failure to follow contractual requirements— relying on concepts such as waiver of the procedural requirements and oral modification of the contract. For example, in *Lewistown Miller Construction Co. v. Martin*, the project was a custom hunting camp and the owner ordered the contractor to make numerous additions and modifications to the project.[4] Although there was a provision in the contract that all changes had to be in writing, the court held that the owner had waived the written change order requirement by making payments on the changes and accepting the work performed. Reliance on these doctrines is risky, however,

---

4   271 P.3d 48, 52 (Mont. 2011).

because they rely on a court's interpretation of the facts in a particular case.

E.   LIQUIDATED DAMAGES

Liquidated damages clauses are common in construction contracts to address issues of delay. These clauses provide a set amount of damages that will be suffered if the project is delayed beyond the established completion date. In the construction context, the liquidated damages are usually assessed on a per day basis. So, for example, if the contract provides for $500 per day in liquidated damages, and the contractor is 2 days late in completing the project, then the owner can charge $1,000 against the balance due to the contractor. The parties can agree when the liquidated damages stop. Ordinarily liquidated delay damages cease once the project is substantially complete. The EJCDC contracts, however, provides a two tiered approach—with one amount of liquidated damages before substantial completion and a second, lower amount for delay in obtaining final completion.[5]

Liquidated damages are not unique to the construction industry and developed as a method to provide certainty to contracting parties when the actual amount of damages suffered upon a breach would be difficult to ascertain. Courts will enforce these provisions so long as they represent a true attempt to ascertain damages suffered and are not merely a penalty for delay. Courts have adopted two

---

[5]   EJCDC C–520 § 4.03.

approaches to determine whether the liquidated damage amounts are reasonable. The first, and the majority approach is known as the **prospective approach**. Under this approach, the analysis of reasonableness is done at the time the parties entered into the contract, and the question is whether it was a reasonable estimate of anticipated damages—without the benefit of subsequent events. It is irrelevant whether the amounts actually suffered were higher or lower than the actual amounts so long as the basis for calculating was reasonable. The alternative approach is the **retrospective approach** in which the court will consider the reasonableness of the liquidated damage amount in light of the damages *actually suffered*.[6]

From the perspective of those subject to liquidated damages—contractors and subcontractors, these provisions have pros and cons. Often, regardless of the amounts, liquidated damages provisions are viewed as an unfair and unjustified penalty. However, liquidated damages also provide certainty by capping the amount of damages the delaying party is responsible to pay. In fact, if a liquidated damages provision is included in a contract, the party is barred from seeking any damages above the stipulated sum, regardless of the amount of direct or consequential damages suffered as a result of the delay. Subcontractors should be aware that even if their subcontract agreement does not provide for liquidated damages, they may be

---

[6]   24 Williston on Contracts § 65:17 (4th ed.).

subject to such damages pursuant to the flow-down provision in the contract between the owner and contractor.

Enforcement of liquidated damages provisions are problematic when the owner contributes to the delay. In situations where there is a concurrent delay, some courts have refused to enforce the liquidated damages provision at all.[7] Other courts, in what has been called the "modern rule" have apportioned the delay between the owner and contractor and allowed recovery of the amount (percentage) of delay attributable to the contractor.[8] Courts base the more modern rule on the popularity of liquidated damages provisions and the modern adoption of comparative fault.

F.   INSURANCE OBLIGATIONS

If construction contracts function largely to shift risk for potential claims resulting from a project, it should come as no surprise that construction contracts contain a number of provisions regarding insurance. It is important to know precisely what policies a party is agreeing to obtain—because failure to acquire a policy when required may constitute a material breach of contract or result in a party being responsible for costs that should have been covered by an insurance policy. Generally, insurance policies provide indemnification for

---

[7]   General Ins. Co. v. Commerce Hyatt House, 85 Cal. Rptr. 317, 324 (Cal. Ct. App. 1970).

[8]   Calumet Const. Co. v. Metropolitan Sanitary District of Greater Chicago, 533 N.E.2d 453 (Ill. Ct. App. 1988).

amounts that an insured is legally obligated to pay when those losses are caused by events within the scope of coverage of the insurance policy. If a loss is within the scope of coverage, the insurance company is responsible up to the amount of insurance policy limits. Ordinarily an insurance company that has to pay out on a claim has a right of **subrogation**. That means that the insurance company has the right to seek to recover the amounts paid out on the claim from the responsible party. So, for example, if an insurance company has to pay the medical expenses of an insured involved in an automobile accident, the company has the right to seek recovery for those amounts from the negligent party. In the construction context, allowing subrogation could defeat the purpose of having coverage. Therefore, standardized contracts often require a **waiver of subrogation** at least with regard to Commercial General Liability policies. AIA A–2007 § 11.3.5. An insurance company will likely seek an increased premium to agree to waive the right to subrogation.

In addition to setting out what is covered by the policy, policies also include policy **exclusions** and **exceptions**. Policy exclusions are events which are not covered by the policy. For example, Commercial General Liability policies often contain a "your work" exclusion—excluding from policy coverage claims related to solely to defective construction by the contractor. Policy exceptions are coverage events that would normally be excluded but which the insurance company is willing accept under the particular policy often for an increased premium.

Another important general insurance concept is the **additional insured**. An insurance company is only responsible for paying covered losses on behalf of named insureds. Therefore, on a construction project if the contractor is the only insured on a policy, the owner has no right to make a claim for losses that would otherwise be covered (the same is true if the subcontractor's policy with regard to the contractor). To ensure that the owner is also covered, construction contracts require the owner and owner's representative (under the AIA documents the architect) is listed as an additional insured under the policy. AIA A201–2007 § 11.1.4.

Common insurance policies required on a construction project include: **commercial general liability (CGL), builder's risk, workers' compensation**, and **professional liability insurance.** The purpose of the CGL policy is to allocate risks with regard to personal injury and property damage to property other than the project itself (which is likely excluded by the "your work" exclusion). Builder's risk policies are obtained during the course of construction, and cover certain damage to the property while construction is on-going—such as damage caused by fire, wind or vandalism. Workers' compensation insurance is provided to cover injuries to employees that occur in the course and scope of employment. The design professional may be required to maintain professional liability insurance to cover claims of negligence in the provision of architectural services.

CHAPTER 8

DEFECTIVE CONSTRUCTION

A. INTRODUCTION

Construction is **defective** if it either does not conform to contractual requirements or is performed in a manner that falls below the standard of care that is owed. The types of defects are as diverse as the types of construction projects. Work may be performed in an improper manner, the work may have been performed properly but the wrong material used, or the project design may be inadequate.

This chapter addresses the most common types of claims for defective construction that arise in tort and contract. However, it is important to note that there may be other claims available for defective construction that vary by jurisdiction. For example, some claims have been successful under an **Unfair/Deceptive Trade Practices** statute. Often broadly worded to provide protection to consumers, they can encompass construction. Courts typically require evidence of wrongful/deceptive conduct beyond mere defective work to allow these claims. However, if a successful claim can be asserted, the statute may provide for recovery of attorney's fees and possibly some form of penalty/punitive damages for the conduct which would not be available in a breach of contract claim. For example, a Texas court found a violation of their Deceptive Trade Practices Act where the builder made numerous false representations to the owner including statements about the cost of construction and the time for completion.[1]

As an initial matter, for purposes of liability, it is important to distinguish between the **manifestation** of a defect and the defect itself. A manifestation is an indication that something is amiss—cracks appearing in the wall of a house. Distinguishing the manifestation of a defect from the defect itself is important for a couple of reasons. First, the manifestation indicates that the owner will need to identify what the underlying defect is and who is responsible. So, in the example of the cracking wall, it may be that the crack is appearing because of faulty foundation work—and not defective wall installation. Second, a manifestation puts the owner on notice of a potential defect. In most jurisdictions the statute of limitations starts when the owner knew or should have known of the defect. In short, manifestations of defective construction indicate that the owner had notice of a potentially defective condition and has an obligation to investigate and take action.

B.   DEFINING CONSTRUCTION DEFECT

One difficulty that arises in discussing construction "defects" is that the concept is so broad and implicates so many different claimants and claims that it is impossible to capture every possible claim or claimant. The purpose of this chapter is to

---

[1]   Barnett v. Coppell North Texas, Ltd., 123 S.W.3d 804, 822–23 (Tex. Ct. App. 2003).

summarize generally two categories of defects—those that arise because a party breached a contractual obligation and those that arise because a party breached a duty owed to another (negligence).

C. BREACH OF CONTRACT CLAIMS

A party's performance can be defective because it fails to comply with the express or implied contractual obligations assumed.

1. EXPRESS WARRANTIES

Construction may be defective because the party failed to abide by the terms of the contractual agreement. A defect in this sense does not mean the structure is not functional. It means that it was not built pursuant to contract. For example, the contract might have called for a particular type of flooring that was not used. The contractor's work was defective to the extent the wrong flooring was used.

Defective work can be discovered while construction is on-going or after the project is complete. With regard to defective work discovered during the construction phase, standard contracts have a provisions stating that the contractor agrees to correct the work and bear the cost of correction.[2] Upon substantial completion there is a one year warranty period. During the warranty period the owner has an obligation to give notice to the

---

[2]   AIA A201–2007 § 12.1.1.

contractor of the defective work and an opportunity to cure which the contractor must do within a reasonable time.[3] If the owner does not give notice and an opportunity to cure then the owner waives the right to assert a claim against the contractor. If, on the other hand, the contractor fails to correct the work within a reasonable time, the owner can correct the work and charge it to the contractor. After this contractually agreed to term, the owner has no obligation to give notice to the contractor before correcting work and must rely on the general standard of workmanship when asserting a claim.

One particular express warranty that is included in all standard contracts is a provision regarding quality of work. The AIA contract between the owner and contractor provides: "Work will conform to the requirements of the Contract Documents and will be free from defects, except for those inherent in the quality of the work the Contract Documents require or permit. Work, materials, or equipment not conforming to these requirements may be considered defective."[4]

The owner may believe that the design professional has a contractual obligation to spot and stop defective construction, and that the failure to do so constitutes a breach of contract. Design professionals, on the other hand, want to make it clear that their obligation in the administration of the project is not to direct how the project is

---

[3]   AIA A201–2007 § 12.2.2.1.

[4]   AIA A201–2007 § 3.5.

constructed (what the AIA standard contract describes as the "means, methods, techniques, sequences and procedures" of construction[5]), but simply to observe the construction when the architect visits the site and ensure that construction is proceeding consistent with contract documents. Certainly the parties can agree that the design professional will do more—even up to assuming responsibility to be on site full-time observing and inspecting the work. A design professional involved in the day to day construction process is often called a **clerk-of-the-works**, and courts will look to the language the parties use to establish the scope of the design professionals obligation. Obligations such as "supervise" or "inspect" will place more obligation on the design professional than "observe" or "visit."[6] Of course, even the obligation merely to "observe" places an obligation on the design professional to make reasonable inspection of the work, and imposes liability for failure to do so. As one court observed: "That exhaustive, continuous on-site inspections were not required, however, does not allow the architect to close his eyes on the construction site, refrain from engaging in any inspection procedure whatsoever, and then disclaim liability for construction defects that even the most perfunctory monitoring would have prevented."[7] Regardless of the amount of job-site responsibility

---

[5]   AIA B101–2007 § 3.6.1.2. See also EJCDC C–700 ¶ 9.02.

[6]   AIA B101–2007 § 3.6.2.1 (architect obligated to "visit" at intervals to "observe[ ]" work).

[7]   First National Bank of Akron v. Cann, 503 F.Supp. 419, 436 (N.D. Ohio 1980).

assumed, design professionals still have a responsibility to report back to the owner if they become aware of defective construction, and failure to do so is a breach of contract and possibly professional malpractice as well.

2. IMPLIED WARRANTIES

Even if the contract does not explicitly set out a standard of quality, courts impose one. The implied obligation is to perform in a **"good and workmanlike" manner** which is defined as "that quality of work performed by one who has the knowledge, training, or experience necessary for the successful practice of a trade or occupation and performed in a manner generally considered proficient by those capable of judging such work."[8]

The obligation to perform in a workmanlike manner is implied to all contracts—whether residential or commercial. In the residential context, most jurisdictions also impose a **warranty of habitability** on builders and developers. A general statement of the elements to establish a breach: (1) purchase of a new residence from a builder or developer; (2) latent defect; (3) defect manifested after purchase (purchaser not on notice at time of closing); (4) defect caused by improper construction or design; and (5) defect "created a question of safety or made the house unfit for human habitation."[9] With regard to the first element, whether the

---

[8] Melody Home Mfg. Co. v. Barnes, 741 S.W.2d 349 (Tex. 1987).

[9] Davencourt v. Davencourt, 221 P.3d 234 (Utah 2009).

warranty is limited to the first purchaser or flows to subsequent purchasers depends on the jurisdiction's view of the economic loss rule. If the jurisdiction continues a strict adherence to the rule, the warranty would not protect subsequent purchasers because they have no contractual relationship with the builder.

To give an example, a Texas court found a violation of the implied warranty where the fireplace in a residence was negligently constructed causing the house to catch fire when the fire place was used. The court rejected the builder's argument that it had assumed no such warranty in the construction contract and any warranty assumed was terminated when the purchaser took the deed.[10] The justification for imposing such a warrant is based in public policy concerns. Builders are in a better position to know about latent defects and purchasers often making huge investments, rely builders to construct a habitable structure.[11]

D. TORT CLAIMS

If there is no contract between the parties or if a party to a contract is asserting something other than purely economic loss—such as to personal injury or personal property—a party may bring a tort claim for negligence. The elements of a negligence claim are: (1) duty; (2) breach; (3) causation; and (4) damages.

---

[10]   Humber v. Morton, 426 S.W.2d 554 (Tex. 1968).

[11]   Sloat v. Matheny, 625 P.2d 1031 (Colo. 1981).

In a design-bid-build project delivery system the owner contracts separately with a contractor and architect. In this scenario the architect's actions at the design or contract administration stage could cause a contractor to suffer damages. A contractor relies on the design and specifications prepared by the architect to prepare its bid, and defective drawings can cause the bid to be skewed. During the course of the contract administration the design professional's actions can also cause increased costs to the contractor failing to timely respond to submittals. There is no uniform rule regarding whether the contractor can bring a negligence claim against the design professional in these situations. Some courts will allow a contractor to proceed on the tort claim finding that the architect owes an independent duty to the contractor[12], while others hold that the claim is barred by the economic loss rule.[13]

A contractor may bring suit against the design professional for **negligent misrepresentation** for defective drawings and specifications. The basis of this claim is that the design documents are representations of their adequacy. If the contractor is not able to complete the project because the design professional recommends that the owner terminate the contractor, the contractor may bring a tort claim for **negligent/intentional interference with contract**—the contract between the owner

---

[12]   Donnelly Const. Co. v. Oberg, 677 P.2d 1292 (Ariz. 1984).

[13]   Captiva Lake Investments, LLC v. Ameristructure, Inc., 436 S.W.3d 619 (Mo. Ct. App. 2014).

and contractor. Once again, however, jurisdictions split over whether these are valid tort claims or barred by the economic loss rule.

E. DEFENSES

1. STATUTE OF LIMITATIONS

A defense to a claim of defective construction is that the party waited too late to bring the claim. All states have **statutes of limitation** that set out a specified amount of time to bring a claim. Often the time for bringing a claim in tort and contract are different, and the limitations periods vary dramatically from state to state. The general rule is that the statute of limitation **accrues** or begins to run on both contract and tort claims when the defect is, or should have been, discovered. Often this is when there is a manifestation of the defect. This is known as the **discovery rule**.

2. STATUTE OF REPOSE

The discovery rule for the running of the statute of limitations creates significant problems for builders. Defects may not manifest until years and years after construction is complete. Therefore, for a potentially indefinite period of time the contractor must keep the project on its books and as a potential liability for insurance purposes. To alleviate this uncertainty, states have passed **statutes of repose**. These statutes set out a certain amount of time from occupancy (or some other time at or near completion) and say that all claims after that time are barred. While this provides certainty for builders it is also a harsh rule for the owner. If the defect manifests after the statute of repose has passed (which would start the running of the statute of limitations)—the claim is barred. Statutes often balance these concerns by adopting a statute of repose period that is longer than the statute of limitations, which provides a reasonable amount of time for defects to manifest after construction before the statute bars the claim.

CHAPTER 9

ECONOMIC LOSS RULE

The purpose of the **Economic Loss Rule** is to maintain the distinction between tort and contract rights and remedies. While this might be a noble goal in theory, the rule has been applied to deny damages in a seemingly arbitrary manner and has been manipulated and ignored to allow damages that a strict interpretation would not justify. The rule has also been riddled with exceptions so that the rule has little continuing relevance. Therefore, while it is possible to set out the general contours of the rule, the reality is that jurisdictions vary greatly in how (and when) they apply it.

A. A STATEMENT OF THE RULE

The Economic Loss Rule is intended to stand guard and prevent claims that should be brought in contract from being asserted as a tort claim. The Rule bars a claimant from recovering "purely economic losses from a defendant with whom the claimant did not have contractual privity unless the claimant suffered personal injury or physical property damage."[1] The California Supreme Court in *Seely v. White Motor C.* first articulated the Rule.[2] The underlying purpose is to prevent someone who entered into a contract—with express contractual obligations and liability limitations—

---

[1]   A. Elizabeth Patrick, et al., *Annotated Construction Law Glossary*, p. 68 (ABA 2010).

[2]   403 P.2d 145 (Cal. 1965).

from turning to tort and circumventing those contractual provisions.

B.   DEFINING ECONOMIC LOSS

Economic losses are those losses suffered as the result of the defective or insufficient performance of another, such as the cost to repair/replace or diminution in value due to defective work. To give a simple example, if an owner contracts with a contractor to construct a house and the contractor negligently installs the roof, the owner must sue the contractor for breach of an express or implied provision of the contract, and will be limited to the cost to repair the roof (breach of contract damages). If the owner asserted a "negligent construction" claim instead of a breach of contract claim, the economic loss rule would require dismissal of that tort claim. Economic losses are distinct from personal injury harms or harms to property other than that which was subject to the contract. The economic loss doctrine does not bar claims for personal injury or for harm to other property. Therefore, in our prior example, if the owner was injured by a piece of roofing because of the defective construction, the owner could bring a claim against the contractor for negligence.

C.   CLAIMS FOR PERSONAL INJURY OR "OTHER PROPERTY"

The economic loss rule does not bar tort recovery for personal injury or damage to other property. The basis for this is that these harms are considered distinct from the agreed to contractual performance. Personal injuries contemplated here are bodily harms to an individual. It is important to note that, even if a personal injury claim is not barred by the economic loss rule, the claimant still has the obligation to prove the elements of a negligence claim (duty, breach, causation, and damages) before the defendant will be liable.

The more difficult issue is the definition of "other property." Courts have taken two approaches to identify "other" property—that is property which is not the subject of contractual performance. The first view is known as the **integrated product** or **integrated structure** approach, and considers all components of a structure to be the "product" for purposes of the economic loss rule. For example, when a defectively installed sprinkler system caused damage to the flowing and subflooring—the claim against the sprinkler installer in tort was dismissed because the court held that all integrated parts of the building made up the structure and did not recognize the flooring as "other property" as compared to the sprinkler system.[3] The second approach is the **component product** approach. Under this approach, the component parts of a structure is considered "other property." Therefore, in the prior example, the owner would be able to sue the sprinkler subcontractor because the system damaged the flooring—"other property."

---

[3] Lockheed Martin Corp. v. RFI Supply, Inc., 440 F.3d 549, 555 (1st Cir. 2006).

D. ECONOMIC LOSS RULE IN CONSTRUCTION CONTEXT

The economic loss rule is relevant to every relationship in the construction context because of the inter-related connections between those with and without contracts. To analyze whether the economic loss rule would bar recovery in a particular circumstance, the starting point is whether there is a contract between the parties. If the answer is yes, then the economic loss rule requires the claim for defective construction must be brought in contract unless there are personal injuries or harm to other property. Therefore, an owner cannot sue a subcontractor for breach of contract for the subcontractor's defective work on a project. Similarly, the subcontractor cannot sue the owner for damages incurred by the subcontractor as a result of owner-caused delays. From the tort perspective, the owner would not be able to sue the subcontractor in negligence if there was no personal injury or harm to property other than the contract. If the economic loss rule applied then the owner would be limited to suing the contractor for the actions of the subcontractor and the contractor could then seek recovery from the subcontractor.

Claims against design professionals raise different concerns and require additional analysis. Because design professionals are professionals and assume an obligation (duty) to the owner as a result of their professional status independent of their contractual relationship, the owner may be able to bring both a claim of breach of contract and a negligence (malpractice) claim.[4] However, not all courts agree with this approach. For example, the Arizona Supreme Court held that the broader professional-status obligations were subsumed into the contract between the owner and the design professional and therefore the economic loss rule barred a tort claim based on defective design.[5]

The actions (or inactions) of design professionals can have a significant impact not just on the owner, but on every participant in the construction process—particularly contractors and subcontractors. The general rule is that the contractor/subcontractors have no claim against design professionals because they have no contract and claims based on delay or inadequate plans and specifications would be purely economic losses.[6] However, some courts have been willing to allow claims based on **negligent misrepresentations** made by the design professional through the design documents. The Restatement (Second) of Torts recognizes an independent cause of action for misrepresentation despite the lack of privity where a party negligently supplies information that others will rely upon and some courts have been willing to impose this duty on the design professional.[7]

---

[4]   Business Men's Assurance Co. v. Graham, 891 S.W.2d 438 (Mo. Ct. App. 1995).

[5]   Flagstaff Affordable Housing Ltd. v. Design Alliance, Inc., 223 P.3d 664, 672 (Ariz. 2010).

[6]   Berschauer/Phillips Constr. Co. v. Seattle School Dist. No. 1, 881 P.2d 986 (Wash. 1994)

[7]   Restatement (Second) of Torts § 552.

CHAPTER 10

DAMAGES AND DISPUTE RESOLUTION

A. TYPES OF DAMAGES

1. CONTRACT DAMAGES

Keep in mind as you contemplate calculation of damages in the construction context that construction—no matter how complex—will ordinarily operate through the familiar lens of contract law. Therefore, just as in any other contractual relationship, when a party breaches a construction contract, the goal is to give the nonbreaching party the **benefit of the bargain** they struck.[1] The damages awarded to satisfy the benefit of the bargain are known as **expectation damages**. This in essence means that the goal in a contract dispute is to put the non-breaching party in the same position she would have been if she had received adequate performance. In addition to these direct damages, the law also allows the non-breaching party to recover **consequential damages**—those damages that, although not directly the result of the breach, were reasonably foreseeable at the time the contract was entered into.

Three aspects of the construction industry make analyzing damages challenging. First is that that parties suffer unique damages. So, for example, in

---

[1]   Restatement (Second) of Contracts § 347.

the typical design-bid-build contract the owner enters into a contract with a design professional. If the design professional breaches their contract by producing a defective design, the owner may have to hire a new designer to redesign a portion of the project and may have to pay to have defective work remedied if part of the defective design was actually constructed. On the other hand, if the owner breaches its contract with the design professional— for example by failing to pay for the services—the designer's damages are most likely only the fee due under the contract. These are very different claims for damages—both in type and amount. The second challenge is that damages can be difficult to isolate and calculate with certainty because they occur in the course of an on-going project where the harm caused can be the fault of a number of participants. The problem of separating out responsibility for concurrent liability can be particularly difficult in the context of delay damages. Third, claims for damages must always be considered in light of the construction contract, which will attempt to limit damages or shift the risk of loss. Contractual provisions limit the damages that the traditional rules of contract would allow. Finally, the economic loss doctrine can prohibit recovery even when a party has suffered damages.

2.   TORT DAMAGES

In addition to damages for breach of a contract, a party may bring a claim in tort. Tort claims comprise both negligent and intentional conduct. Tort law allows recovery where a harm has been done, but there is no agreement between the parties. To establish a negligence claim, the plaintiff must establish that the defendant owed the plaintiff a duty, breached that duty, and caused the harm that damaged the plaintiff. The damages that a plaintiff can recover in a tort claim are broader than contract damages because the party is not limited to the benefit of the bargain and because the parties have not negotiated to shift risk of loss as they have in a contractual relationship. Damages that are recoverable include compensatory damages including general and special damages. The economic loss rule limits the ability of an individual to bring a claim in tort when asserting a claim for contract damages.

3.   QUASI CONTRACTUAL DAMAGES

A breach of contract claim—and the resultant benefit of the bargain damages—presumes the existence of a valid and enforceable contract. It may be that the claimant is seeking compensation where the parties never entered into a contract. In these situations, the non-breaching party is not entitled to contract or tort damages, but may be able to recover restitution. Unlike a breach of contract claim in which the law allows the non-breaching party to recover expectation damages, recovery under a quasi-contract is intended to retrieve the value of the benefit received or the value of the services provided. If a contract exists, then quasi contractual remedies are not available.

a. Promissory Estoppel

A party may be able to recovery if they can establish **promissory estoppel**. Here, the claimant asserts that a party should be held to its promise because a promise was made, the claimant relied on the promise, and the reliance was reasonable. For example, when a contractor relies on the quote of a subcontractor in submitting a bid, courts have held that although there is no enforceable contract between the contractor and the subcontractor, the contractor can hold the subcontractor to its bid on the basis of promissory estoppel. If the subcontractor refuses to honor its quote, the contractor can have the work performed by another and can recover from the subcontractor the difference between the original quote and the cost to have the work done by the substitute.

b. Unjust Enrichment

The second extra-contractual claim is **unjust enrichment**. These are situations where one party performed work which was accepted and which was performed with the expectation of payment, and which the receiving party should not unjustly be enriched by keeping the work without paying for it. If a claim for unjust enrichment is proven, the measure of damages is the value of the item conferred upon the recipient. In the construction context the amount the claimant is allowed to recover is the increase in value of the property by the improvement.[2] The presence of a contract will

---

[2] Bruner & O'Connor on Construction Law § 19:37.

defeat a claim for unjust enrichment. So most courts would not allow a subcontractor to bring a claim against the owner (even though the owner has received the benefit of the subcontractor's work) because of the presence of the contract with the contractor. Other courts, however, look to see whether the owner has paid the contractor for the subcontractor's work. If the contractor has been paid, then the subcontractor's claim is defeated, but if the contractor has not been paid then the subcontractor can pursue its unjust enrichment claim.[3]

c. Quantum Meruit

The third extra-contractual measure of damages is **quantum meruit**. These damages are available where the claimant performed services, the recipient was aware of and approved of the improvement, and it was reasonable for the claimant to expect payment. If a party is entitled to quantum meruit they can recover the value of the services provided.

B.   DAMAGES MUST BE ESTABLISHED WITH REASONABLE CERTAINTY

In calculating damages, the party asserting the right to damages bears the burden of establishing with reasonable certainty the amount of damages suffered. In some situations this is an easy calculation, and is merely the difference between

---

[3]   Wang Elec., Inc. v. Smoke Tree Resort, LLC, 283 P.3d 45 (Ariz. Ct. App. 2012).

the contract price agreed to and how much it actually cost the non-breaching party. Thus, if a subcontractor fails to fully perform its scope of work, and the contractor has to retain a substitute, the contractor's damages are the difference between the original contract amount and the cost to perform the work. When damages are incurred because of delays or increased work the non-breaching party has the obligation of establishing damages with reasonable certainty. Sometimes this is a straight-forward calculation—the non-breaching party may be able to point to increases in labor or material, rental costs of idle equipment, increased home office overhead because of additional time spent on the job. In these situations the calculation of damages is straight-forward. Rarely, however, are damage calculations so clearly defined and the method for calculating and determining the amount of damages suffered can be a challenge.

C.   DETERMINING EXPECTATION DAMAGES

This section discusses damages recoverable by the owner, design professional, and contractor. When discussing recover for breach of contract, there is a presumption that there was no material breach by the claimant. If the claimant is guilty of a material breach then the other party is entitled to stop work and the claimant is not entitled to damages. It also bears repeating that this section discusses the damages that are available generally and contractual provisions may limit or eliminate the right to recover for some categories of damage.

1.   OWNER DAMAGES

The owner's contractual relationship varies by the type of project delivery system, but traditionally the owner will contract with a design professional and a contractor. The owner retains the design professional to prepare the design documents and the contractor to perform the work. With regard to the design professional, the owner is entitled to a design that meets the minimum standard of care in the relevant design industry. If the design professional does not perform at all or only partially performs, the owner is entitled to a return of any fees paid. If the design was prepared but was defective, the owner is entitled to the amounts required to make the project comply with minimum design specifications. These are the direct damages caused by the breach. The owner may also be able to recover any damages that arise as a foreseeable consequence of the breach. For example, if a defective design delays the owner obtaining rental income from the structure, this lost income is recoverable as a foreseeable consequential damage.

The design professional's obligations to the owner run not only in contract but also in tort, and the owner may have a claim for professional malpractice against the designer. To recover, the owner will have to establish the elements of negligence: duty, breach, causation, and damage. The types of damages (direct and consequential) as well as the calculation of damages is the same in the malpractice case as in the breach of contract case. The difference is that, if the tort claim succeeds, any contractual limitations that exist on the breach of contract case are not applicable and may justify imposition of punitive damages.

The owner's expectation interest with regard to the contractor is to complete the project on time, for the agreed to price, and in a good workmanlike (non-defective) manner. Therefore, if the contractor fails to meet any of these three expectations the owner is entitled to the direct and consequential damages suffered. Consequential damages for late completion could include increased fees to the design professional for additional administration services or a lost favorable interest rate on a loan. If the contractor fails to complete the scope of work agreed to in the contract or fails to complete the project at all, the owner is entitled to have the project finished and then recover the direct cost of completion from the contractor as well as any consequential damages suffered. Finally, if the contractor breaches the duty to perform in a good and workmanlike manner, the owner may recover the cost to remedy the work, and any consequential damages suffered.

Generally owners are entitled to sufficient damages to put them in the position they would have been in if the contract had been performed. There are two methods for calculating these damages with regard to defective construction. First is the cost of **repair or replacement**. This is the generally accepted method of calculating damages, and is simply the cost the owner either has or would sustain to make the structure comply with the contract. However, in certain situations, allowing repair/replacement damages would be disproportionate to the nature of the breach. For example, where the contractor has substantially complied with the contract and the cost of remedying the defect would require destruction of work already completed or where the cost of repair greatly exceeds the contracted for cost of construction. If the contractor were required to absorb the cost of demolishing work to remedy a defect then the owner would recover more than the benefit of her bargain. In these situations courts will often deny recovery of repair/replacement damages and instead award the owner the **diminution in value**.[4] It is often said that diminution is awarded instead of repair costs to avoid **economic waste**. Diminution in value damages are calculated by awarding the owner the difference between the fair market value of the property as constructed and as contracted for.

The classic example of where diminution is appropriate is *Jacob & Youngs, Inc. v. Kent*.[5] In *Kent* the construction contract required the contractor to use pipe in the house manufactured by "Reading." Much of the pipe used, although of equal quality to Reading, was not manufactured by Reading. The owner sued for breach of contract, and sought demolition of much of the structure that had already been completed so the piping could be replaced. Judge Cardozo, writing for the New York

---

[4]   Restatement (Second) of Contracts § 348, cmt. c.

[5]   129 N.E. 889 (N.Y. Ct. App. 1921).

court, while recognizing that the contractor breached the contract by installing improper pipes, would not allow the owner to recover the replacement costs. Instead, the court awarded the owner the difference in value of the property as contracted (with Reading pipe) and as constructed.

In certain situations the economic waste doctrine will not bar recovery of repair/replacement costs. First is where the breach by the contractor is in bad faith (or a willful failure to perform according to the contract). Second, when the structure is unsafe as built and repair/replacement is necessary to make it safe. Finally, other situations such as where the structure as built cannot be used for its intended purpose or where the defective portion of work goes to the essence of the underlying contract (*e.g.* unique aesthetic aspects) repair damages may be appropriate.

Under traditional contract principles, the owner is entitled both to the damages that flow directly from the breach itself (cost of repair, increased administration costs) as well as consequential damages which are damages that are a foreseeable consequence of the breach. A common consequential damage that owners often seek is lost profits. If the business is established and the profits that were lost can be established with reasonable certainty they are recoverable; however, difficulties arise when a new business seeks lost profits. If the new business cannot establish with reasonable certainty then lost profits are not recoverable.

The owner can recover similar damages when the design professional breaches a contractual or professional duty to the owner. With regard to the design scope of work, breach would include the damages suffered as a result of the incomplete or inadequate design. For contract administration, the owner can recover damages that results from the breach of the duty to reasonably inspect the on-going work or approving payment for work that was not actually completed. The own can also recover to the extent the design professional approves materials not in compliance with the contract documents. In all of these situations the owner can recover the direct and consequential damages suffered (limited by any contractual provisions). To the extent the architect is liable for defective construction, the owner can recover the cost to repair/replace or the diminution in value (with the same limitations regarding economic waste).

2.   DESIGN PROFESSIONAL DAMAGES

The design professional enters into a contract to perform design work and expects to be paid the contract amount for the work. If the owner fails to pay the contractual amount, the design professional is entitled to the contract amount. Consequential damages incurred due to a breach by the owner are also recoverable. In addition, the design professional may claim that certain services provided were beyond the scope of the original contract (in AIA parlance was "additional services") and that the designer is entitled to additional compensation for the extra work. If it is determined that in fact the work is beyond what was contractually agreed to, then the design professional is entitled to the amount of services rendered.

3.   CONTRACTOR DAMAGES

The contractor's expectation with the owner is that the contractor will receive the contract amount for completing the project in accordance with the contract documents. The analysis of contractor damages in this chapter also applies to claims by a subcontractor. The contractor expects she will be able to follow and rely on the plans and specifications provided by the owner, and will be compensated for any additional work that has to be performed as a result of defective drawings/ specifications.

If the owner fails to make the required payment for work performed then the contractor can sue for the amounts due under the contract and consequential damages suffered. If the contractor is required (either because of changes implemented by the owner or because of defective design documents) to perform work beyond that agreed to in the contract, the contractor is entitled to recover for the additional work performed. The most complicated element of damage occurs when the contractor's work is made inefficient by the actions of the owner. Here, inefficient means that work was made more expensive than it would have been without the unjustified interference or disruption. The classic example if the situation where the contractor was scheduled to perform work in warm (or dry) weather and pushed into cold (or wet) weather which increases the contractor's cost to perform the work. The contractor is entitled to compensation for the additional cost incurred because of the inefficiencies.

In many situations, however, it can be very difficult for the contractor to establish the precise amount of damages caused by the loss of productivity throughout the course of a construction project. Over time methods have been established for the contractor to estimate the amount of damages suffered by the contractor which are compensable. Because these are estimates, the approaches have varying degrees of reliability.

a. Measured Mile

The **measured mile** method is the most reliable and preferred approach yet it is also the hardest to use. The contractor identifies a portion of the project similar to the affected portion and compares the time to completion of the delayed and undelayed portion which provides the amount of disruption attributable to the owner. At that point the number of hours can be multiplied by an hourly rate—to put a dollar value on the inefficiencies caused by the owner. The difficulty is finding a sufficiently similar portion of the project to provide the comparison.

b. Should-Cost

The **should-cost** approach is a method of establishing damages by comparing the time to complete a portion of work on the current project and comparing it to similar work on other projects. In other words, what the work should have cost but-for the delay. Courts are skeptical of this approach and put the burden on the contractor to demonstrate its reliability.

c. Industry Studies

Certain industry groups in the construction industry prepare **industry studies** estimating the amount of delay that will be caused by various conditions. Contractors may use these studies to establish how certain delays typically impact projects and analogize it to the current project. These studies have been challenged as both biased because they were prepared by industry groups and as unreliable because the calculations do not take into account the conditions of *this* job site. The contractor has a very high burden to establish that these average delays reasonably correspond to the conditions on the project.

d. Total Cost

The **total cost method** is the simplest for the contractor to use. Here, the contractor simply takes the total amount of costs incurred on the project and subtracts the original bid amount. The difference is put forward as the amount of disruption damages suffered over the course of the project. The underlying assumptions of this approach make its reliably extraordinarily suspect. It assumes that all delays and costs throughout the project were the fault of the owner—and none of the delays are attributable to the contractor. It also assumes that the contractor's original bid was reasonable.

e. Modified Total Cost

The **modified total cost method** attempts to alleviate some of the concerns raised by the total cost method. This method takes into account and subtracts out from the amount due the costs attributable to the contractor.

f. Jury Verdict

The **jury verdict method** of calculating delay damages is poorly named. A better name for the approach might be the "no better method" approach. Under this method the court evaluates all available evidence and makes a determination of damages based on the evidence presented. To use this method, the contractor must show that he clearly suffered delay damages and that no other method provides a better more reliable estimation of the damages. Owners challenge this approach on the basis that it is nothing more than speculation and does not satisfy the requirement that damages must be proven with reasonable certainty.

D. DEFENSES

1. MITIGATION OF DAMAGES

As in all contractual relationships, the party alleging the breach of a construction contract has an obligation to **mitigate** its damages. This means that the party must take steps to protect the property or structure, or risk being denied recovery for any additional damages caused due to the failure to mitigate. For example, if the owner is alleging that the contractor defectively installed a roof and it leaks, if the owner does nothing to correct or contain the leaks and then seeks recovery from the contractor, a court may deny the owner the right to recover for damages that could have been avoided if the owner had taken reasonable steps to mitigate the damages.

2. BETTERMENT

The **betterment** doctrine is not unique to the construction industry, but it is a common defense raised by design professionals when faced with a claim for damages by an owner. The defense arises when the design documents omit a necessary component, and as a result the owner incurs additional cost to complete the project. In these situations, the owner will argue that the design professional should be responsible for the increase. The problem with the owner's argument, however, is that she would have been responsible for the higher cost if the design was correct and therefore, while the design professional may be responsible for the cost of tearing out the inappropriate product, they are not responsible for the increased cost of the new material because the owner would have been responsible for those amounts if the project had been designed correctly.

In contract terms, the owner should be made whole as a result of the defective design, but should not be put in a better position than she would have been had the design been correct. A good example of the doctrine in action is *St. Joseph Hospital v. Corbetta Const. Co., Inc.*, 316 N.E.2d 51 (Ill. Ct. App. 1974). The owner retained an architectural firm to design a hospital. The design called for wall paneling that did not comply with Chicago building code requirements. The deficiency was not discovered until after the paneling was installed and rejected by a city inspector. The owner had the deficient paneling removed and code-compliant paneling installed. The owner alleged that the architect was responsible for the demolition costs to remove the old paneling and the increased cost of the more expensive code-compliant paneling. The court allowed the owner to recover the cost of removing the old paneling, but not the increased cost of the new paneling because the owner *should* have paid the cost of the new paneling and did not solely because the design was defective. To allow the owner to recover the additional cost from the architect would allow the owner to obtain a product better than what he contracted to receive.

3.   CONTRACTUAL LIMITATIONS

Throughout this book various contractual doctrines have been discussed that operate as defenses to damage claims. These include clauses that provide no damage for delay but merely additional time, waivers of consequential damages, and indemnification provisions.

E.   DISPUTE RESOLUTION

The construction project without some dispute is like a four-leaf clover—often hoped for but rarely seen. Therefore, standard construction contracts set out a mechanism for resolving disputes. The resolution process is actually a two stage process. First is the recognition of a dispute and second, following the informal dispute resolution process provided for in the contract. If the informal process is unsuccessful, resolving disputes either through arbitration or litigation.

1.   INFORMAL DISPUTE
RESOLUTION PROCESS

Once a dispute arises over a claim for additional compensation or additional time, the AIA contract contemplates that dispute will be presented to the Initial Decision Maker—either someone agreed to by the parties or the architect. The Initial Decision Maker then must review the claim and issue a decision that either resolves the claim or that states the decision maker is unable to reach a decision.[6] The decision of the initial decision maker must (a) be in writing; (b) set out the reasons for the finding; and (c) identify how the time or cost of the contract will be modified.[7] Either party may then seek non-binding mediation of the decision within thirty days of the decision. If no request is filed the parties agree to waive the right to assert the claim in

---

[6]   AIA A201–2007 § 15.2.2.

[7]   AIA A201–2007 § 15.2.4.

subsequent mediation or arbitration.[8] The rationale for including this in-project resolution process is to provide finality for those claims not pursued, and to avoid the difficulties of establishing claims when the project is complete.

2.   FORMAL DISPUTE RESOLUTION

In the event the parties cannot resolve disputes in mediation, the parties may pursue formal resolution of their disputes in either arbitration or litigation. The AIA documents no longer default to arbitration as the formal dispute resolution process, but contemplate that the parties will choose either arbitration or litigation.

a. Arbitration

Arbitration is a longstanding and well-accepted method of resolving construction disputes. Three primary justifications have been put forth for preferring arbitration over litigation in construction disputes. First, participants in a construction project need quick resolution and finality in decisions. Allowing claims to linger or face multiple appeals/remands that could happen in litigation keeps a completed project open and lingering when the parties would prefer to close the books on the project and move on. Second, the cost of arbitration is perceived to be less than the cost of litigation. Third, because construction claims are complex, utilizing arbitrators familiar with the construction process and construction contracts is better for the

---

[8]   AIA A201–2007 § 15.2.6.1.

parties than relying on a lay jury or generalist judge to decide disputes. Of course these are broad generalizations and all of these justifications do not exist on every project.

Arbitration must be included in the party's contract and a party cannot be forced to arbitrate a claim outside the scope of the arbitration agreement. Historically, a party could revoke the arbitration provision and proceed to litigation; however, with passage of the **Federal Arbitration Act (FAA)** and its state equivalents, if a party agrees to arbitration, they cannot subsequently revoke the agreement.[9] The FAA established a strong preference in favor of enforcing arbitration agreements and provides that if a lawsuit is filed on a claim subject to an arbitration provision, then the case should be stayed if a party seeks to enforce an arbitration provision.[10] The **American Arbitration Association (AAA)** recommends the following arbitration provision: "Any controversy or claim arising out of or relating to this contract, or breach thereof, shall be settled by arbitration administered by the American Arbitration Association under its Construction Industry Arbitration Rules, and judgment on the award rendered by the arbitrator(s) may be entered in any court having jurisdiction thereof." Notice that this is a broad provision that includes all claims related to the project, but parties are free to modify and limit the claims subject to arbitration.

---

[9]   9 U.S.C. § 2.

[10]   9 U.S.C. § 3.

It is important to recognize that obligation to arbitrate is established as a matter of contractual agreement and just as other contractual provisions can be waived, so can the right to demand arbitration. The general rule is that if a party acts inconsistent with an intent to enforce the arbitration agreement it will be waived. Therefore, where a party engages in litigation without demanding arbitration, a court may find those actions waived the right to demand arbitration.[11]

Once it is determined that a claim is subject to an arbitration provision, the next question is the number and method of selecting arbitrators, where the arbitration will be held, and the law to be applied in the arbitration. These are all issues that the parties should agree to contractually. Often, the contract will provide that the claims will be subject to a particular set of rules—for example, the AAA Construction Industry Arbitration Rules. The number of arbitrators is usually one or three. Of course, there are costs associated with arbitration which can be substantial—including a filing fee that increases incrementally based on the size of the project and the arbitrator(s)' fee which is usually split between the parties.

The arbitration process itself is stream-lined and intended to resolve disputes in a timely manner. To this end, there is very little discovery allowed and very few depositions taken. The rules of evidence and the rules of civil procedure do not apply. The

---

[11]   North West Michigan Constr., Inc. v. Stroud, 462 N.W.2d 804, 805 (Mich. Ct. App. 1990).

arbitrator will hold a hearing and allow the parties to present their evidence. The AIA documents allow for consolidation of arbitration and joinder of parties to the arbitration if certain conditions are so that as many issues as possible can be resolved in one arbitration.[12] Afterward the arbitrator, within a set amount of time, will issue an award. The arbitrator is not obligated to provide justifications for the decision, and lack of detail is not a basis for challenging the award. Once an arbitration award if final, it is enforceable in court as other judgments.

The bases for challenging an arbitrator's award under the FAA are limited and not likely to be successful. They include: (1) the award was procured by "corruption, fraud, or undue means"; (2) proof of "evident partiality or corruption" of the arbitrator; (3) the arbitrator refused to postpone the hearing where there was good cause or refusing to hear pertinent evidence; or (4) the arbitrator "exceeded their powers."[13] Parties might be tempted to expand this limited basis for challenging an arbitrator's award in their contract. For example, in *Hall Street Associates, LLC v. Mattel, Inc.*, the parties agreement provided that the arbitrator's award could be challenged where the arbitrator's findings of fact were "not supported by substantial evidence" or the conclusions of law were erroneous.[14] The United States Supreme Court rejected the added bases for challenging an arbitration award,

---

[12]   AIA A201–2007 § 15.4.4.

[13]   9 U.S.C. § 10(a).

[14]   552 U.S. 576, 579 (2008).

holding that the statutory bases for challenging an award are exclusive and the parties cannot expand them by agreement.

b. Litigation

If there is no enforceable arbitration provision, parties often turn to litigation to resolve their disputes. If the dispute is litigated, it is treated just as any other claim on the court's civil docket (unless the jurisdiction has provided special procedures for construction litigation). Therefore, the rules of civil procedure, including the requirements of pleadings, discovery, and motion practice, are used to develop the case. While discovery is greatly curtailed in arbitration, all of the discovery mechanisms are available in litigation, which means that the parties will likely be more familiar with the strength and weaknesses of the respective parties' positions. Assuming that claims survive summary judgment, the disputes are then submitted either to a judge or to a jury for determination. The rules of evidence apply to the admission and consideration of evidence. After a decision by the trial court, the parties are entitled to any appeals of right that are available in the civil context. Judgments are final upon the expiration of the time for asserting the last appeal.

INDEX

References are to Pages